CULTURE SMART!
UZBEKISTAN

Alexey Ulko

·K·U·P·E·R·A·R·D·

ISBN 978 1 85733 852 2
This book is also available as an e-book: eISBN 978 1 85733853 9
British Library Cataloguing in Publication Data
A CIP catalogue entry for this book is available from the British Library

First published in Great Britain
by Kuperard, an imprint of Bravo Ltd
59 Hutton Grove, London N12 8DS
Tel: +44 (0) 20 8446 2440 Fax: +44 (0) 20 8446 2441
www.culturesmart.co.uk
Inquiries: sales@kuperard.co.uk

Series Editor Geoffrey Chesler
Design Bobby Birchall

Printed in Malaysia

About the Author

ALEXEY ULKO is a linguist, art critic, filmmaker, and writer who lives in Uzbekistan. A First Class Honors graduate in English Language and Literature from the University of Samarkand, he taught English there for ten years and became the first Hornby Scholar from Uzbekistan to obtain an M.Ed. TTELT degree from the University of St. Mark and St. John, Plymouth, in the UK. Since 2003 he has been an independent consultant in English-language teacher training, a translator, and a writer on contemporary Central Asian culture and art. He has made several short films and spoken at conferences on the subject. He is a member of the Association of Art Historians and the European Society for Central Asian Studies.

The Culture Smart! series is continuing to expand.
For further information and latest titles visit
www.culturesmart.co.uk

The publishers would like to thank **CultureSmart!**Consulting for its help in researching and developing the concept for this series.

CultureSmart!Consulting creates tailor-made seminars and consultancy programs to meet a wide range of corporate, public-sector, and individual needs. Whether delivering courses on multicultural team building in the USA, preparing Chinese engineers for a posting in Europe, training call-center staff in India, or raising the awareness of police forces to the needs of diverse ethnic communities, it provides essential, practical, and powerful skills worldwide to an increasingly international workforce.

For details, visit www.culturesmartconsulting.com

CultureSmart!Consulting and **CultureSmart!** guides have both contributed to and featured regularly in the weekly travel program "Fast Track" on BBC World TV.

contents

contents

Map of Uzbekistan

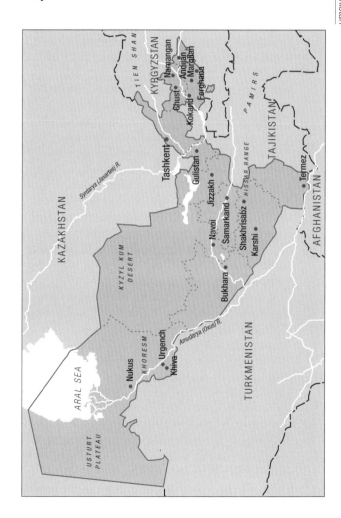

introduction

Uzbekistan, like its Central Asian neighbors, is not particularly well known to the outside world. For about seventy years it was one of the fifteen republics of the USSR, then commonly referred to as "Russia," and few Westerners knew much about the cultural and ethnic differences within this huge country. In 1991, after Independence, Uzbekistan joined the family of other "stans," of which the most internationally prominent are Afghanistan and Pakistan. At the same time, the names of Uzbekistan's oldest cities, Samarkand and Bukhara, are often instantly recognizable and evoke glamorous associations with the Great Silk Road and *The Arabian Nights*. Which of these impressions is the right one? All and none, for Uzbekistan is an exciting mixture of different cultural traditions, from Persian to Turkic, from European and Russian, to the contemporary globalized amalgam.

When you arrive in Uzbekistan you immediately discover how multicultural its society is, which you may see as something to celebrate as well as cause for a certain disappointment.

Those who expect to find a stereotypically drab post-Soviet country with dull concrete buildings and hapless people will be rewarded with the chance to dip into a vibrant, colorful, and exotic Central Asian life. Uzbeks are open, hospitable, emotional, and positive people, but they also like a certain order. Travelers expecting to face the kind of chaos that overwhelms the urban labyrinths of such cities as Cairo or Delhi will be pleasantly surprised by careful city planning, wide tree-lined streets, and well-kept architectural monuments.

On the other hand, visitors should be prepared for some Soviet-style restrictions and bureaucracy and the lack of certain features of the globalized world such as cash machines, McDonald's, Starbucks, and broadband. You will also notice a distinct urban–rural divide and different cultural patterns and rules used in different communities. The ethnic and linguistic mixture may be confusing, but getting to know the people of Uzbekistan can be a hugely enjoyable experience.

This short guide aims to raise awareness of the complexity of Uzbekistan's culture, to equip you with the knowledge of how to make the most of your visit, and to help you to avoid or handle the occasional difficulty. It sets out to guide you through a spectrum of local subcultures, from the traditional rural Uzbek through a mix of Russian, European, and Soviet cultures to the modern cosmopolitan community.

As a native Russian-speaking citizen of Uzbekistan, I am aware of the inevitable subjectivity of my own perspective. To compensate for this bias, I have sought advice from both Uzbek-speaking friends and foreign friends who have spent time in Uzbekistan in different roles and positions. They have shared their insights with me and greatly enriched my own understanding of Uzbek culture.

Welcome to Uzbekistan!

Hush kelibsiz O'zbekistonga!

Key Facts

Official Name	Republic of Uzbekistan	
Capital City	Tashkent	Pop. officially 2.3 million
Main Cities	Samarkand, Bukhara, Namangan, Andijan, Ferghana, Jizzakh, Termez, Navoi, Nukus, Gulistan, Karshi, Urgench	
Population	31.8 million	Overall population density 153 per sq. mile (59 per sq. km)
Area	172,700 sq. miles (447,000 sq. km)	
Border Countries	Afghanistan, Kazakhstan, Kyrgyzstan, Tajikistan, Turkmenistan	The only Central Asian country that has borders with all others
Ethnic Makeup	Uzbek 70%, Russian 5%, Tajik 5%, Karakalpak 3%, Kazakh 2%, others 15%	More than 100 ethnicities
Climate	Sharply continental. Dry, hot summers and mild to cold winters	
Goverment	Presidential republic. Elected for a 5-year term, the president appoints ministers and selects provincial governors.	Bicameral Supreme Assembly (Oliy Majlis), consisting of the Senate and the Legislative Chamber
Literacy	98%	
Languages	Uzbek is the official language. Formerly written in Cyrillic, now also in Latin script.	Russian is the lingua franca. Other minority languages incl. Karakalpak, Tajik, Kazakh.

Religion	Islam 90%, Christianity 7%, others 3%	
Media	State owned. Three national TV plus regional channels broadcast in Uzbek; limited digests in Russian. State radio broadcasts in Uzbek and Russian, and several FM stations broadcast in other local languages.	The main newspapers are the goverment-owned *Xalq So'zi*, and its Russian version, *Narodnoe Slovo*.
Age Structure	Under 15, 35%; 15–65, 60%; over 65, 5%	
Urban and Rural Population	Urban 35%, rural 65%	
Unemployment	Approx. 7%	
GDP Per Capita	US $5,400	
Currency	Uzbek soum (also spelled sum, som)	
Electricity	220 volts, 50 Hz	Round, two-prong plugs, standard European or older Soviet with thinner pins. European plugs will not fit the Soviet sockets, but adapters available.
Internet Domain	.uz	
Telephone	Country code 998	To dial from landline to cell phone, dial 05 + company prefix (90, 91, etc.).
Time Zone	GMT + 5 hrs	No daylight saving

chapter one

LAND & PEOPLE

GEOGRAPHY

Uzbekistan is home to parts of the two largest mountain ranges in Central Asia—the Pamirs and the Tien Shan—but its territorial core is the vast Kyzyl Kum Desert, which lies between the Amudarya (Oxus) and the Syrdarya (Jaxartes) Rivers. One of only two doubly landlocked countries in the world, it has a landmass of 172,700 square miles (447,000 sq. km) and a population of over thirty million, the largest in the region. Only about 10 percent of the land is irrigated—in the river valleys and oases that host its largest cities and most of the population. This has resulted in an extraordinarily uneven distribution of the population: the huge Karakalpak Autonomous Republic in the west occupies 37 percent of the country but has only 5.7 percent of its population, while the fertile Ferghana Valley in the east, a mere 5.1 percent of the territory, is home to about 30 percent of the population.

Mountains make up 23 percent of the total area, the highest peak being Babatag, 14,780 feet (4,668 m) above sea level. However, the mountain ranges, although not particularly high—rarely exceeding 6,000 feet (2,000 m)—split the country into different parts, especially in the south and east, and make traveling between them a bit problematic. They almost completely surround the Ferghana Valley in the

east, as well as the smaller valleys in the south, and form natural barriers between the cities of Jizzakh, Samarkand, and Shakhrisabz. The great Kyzyl Kum Desert lies between Khoresm, an oasis region in the delta of the Amudarya, and the rest of the country. As a result, the rivers, although not easily navigable in recent years, served as natural communication lines for travelers to follow on land, first in their caravans and later by car and train.

The way Uzbekistan was created, and its borders defined, in 1924, reflected the perceived need to give all the newly formed Soviet nations their own land. Drawn up for administrative convenience, and not intended to divide the peoples of the USSR, these borders became a reality in the early 1990s when the newly independent states failed to form a union without travel restrictions. Because the state borders did not coincide with either topography or ethnic makeup, the internal coherence and integrity of transportation was seriously weakened. The Tien Shan range effectively cuts off the Ferghana Valley from the rest of the country, with the only natural access route now going through Tajikistan.

The Hissar range separates the southern province of Surkhandarya from the center. Uzbekistan had to build additional roads and railways to improve connections between Tashkent and Samarkand, Tashkent and Ferghana Valley, and the south of the country and the center, and to streamline the Uzbek part of the Transcaspian Railway. Today, with these problems largely resolved, it is possible to travel from oasis to desert through the mountains in a single trip.

CLIMATE

Uzbekistan has a sharply continental climate with hot, dry summers, unpredictable winter weather, and little precipitation. Most rain falls in the late winter or spring. In summer the average high temperature in June/July may reach 104°F (40°C), but in winter average temperatures do not generally fall below 30°F (-1°C), although at times the low temperature may hit -4°F (-20°C), usually in January/February. The locals believe that the extremely hot and cold spells they call *chillya* ("forty" in Persian) fall on certain dates and last for forty days, but global climate change has made this traditional timetable less than reliable.

Spring and fall tend to be much milder. The weather in March and April is pleasant if unpredictable, and sunny but cold days may alternate with warmer cloudy ones. In May and June the sky is often hazy and the days become increasingly hot. After the summer's heat peaks, the fall arrives with cooler nights, although it may continue to be hot during the day. In October the sky clears and the leaves turn golden, only to be washed off by the gray November rains. Sometimes winter proper starts in December, but increasingly it is January that brings snow and temperatures below zero.

THE ARAL SEA

The Aral Sea, straddling the border of Kazakhstan and Uzbekistan, was the fourth-largest saline lake and inland body of water in the world. Its main sources of water, the Amudarya and the Syrdarya Rivers, are fed by glacial meltwater from the Pamir and Tien Shan Mountains. In the 1960s, the Soviet government started diverting water from these rivers to irrigate the desert around the sea. By 1990, massive irrigation projects had doubled the area under cultivation. Today the combination of water diversion, intensive agriculture, and industrial waste have resulted in a disappearing sea, salinization, organic and inorganic pollution, and extreme environmental degradation.

In 1995, the Nukus Declaration was signed by the Aral Sea Basin countries, aimed at developing a unified approach and cooperation with the international community. Unfortunately, the shrinking sea and salty dust storms have already changed the climate in the region beyond the point of a likely return to stability. With the disappearing sea, there is not sufficient surface area to temper the cold north winds. The sea no longer contributes the moisture it once did to the snowfall in the neighboring and more distant mountains, which in turn reduces the supply of water to the valleys. In the mid-2000s the Aral Sea broke into two smaller basins; so far only some of the water resources of the North Aral, which belongs to Kazakhstan, have been replenished. With the South Aral being primarily in Uzbek territory, the involvement of Uzbekistan is crucial to the rebirth of the Aral Basin as a whole.

The climate tends to be more extreme in the desert and in the mountains. Winters in the Kyzyl Kum Desert are windy and cold, and summers are hot. The hottest area is in the south of the country, where it borders Afghanistan. In recent years global warming and the drying out of the Aral Sea have turned long, snowy winters to shorter ones with less precipitation and greater temperature fluctuation.

THE PEOPLE
Ethnic Makeup
Although Uzbeks make up about 70 percent of the total population, Uzbekistan is ethnically diverse, with sizeable Russian, Tajik, Kazakh, Karakalpak, Korean, Jewish, Armenian, Tartar, and other communities.

Contrary to the official doctrine, which follows the Soviet nationality-building model, the Uzbeks themselves are not an ethnically homogeneous nation, but have different roots and were assembled under one name in the 1920s and '30s. Modern Uzbeks come not only from the Turkic–Mongol nomads who first claimed the name, but also from other Turkic and Persian peoples living within the borders. Over centuries, waves of mostly Turkic-speaking nomadic tribes passed through the area, interspersed with Greeks, Chinese, Arabs, and Mongols. They interacted and mixed with the sedentary population speaking dialects of old Persian. Thus different population groups, dynasties, countries, and cultures emerged and disappeared in the course of history, giving birth to the peoples that, in the early twentieth century, were divided into distinct modern nations.

Today the government is strengthening Uzbek national identity, in order to prevent the ethnic

splintering seen elsewhere. Some people have assimilated with seemingly little concern. Many local Tajiks consider themselves Uzbek, though they retain the Tajik language, of the Persian language family. This may be because they have long shared a common urban lifestyle, which was more of a bond than ethnic or linguistic labels. The Karakalpaks, who live in the desert south of the Aral Sea, have a separate language and tradition closer to Kazakh than Uzbek. Under the Soviet Union they had their own republic, and it remains autonomous within Uzbekistan.

Ethnic Tajiks live compactly in the historical cities of Samarkand and Bukhara, but differ from local Uzbeks only in language (both communities almost universally speak Uzbek, Tajik, and Russian languages, to different extents). Once-nomadic Kazakhs and Kyrgyz form sizeable minorities in Uzbekistan, as well as Irani, Turkmen, and Uighurs, but they are also well integrated with the Uzbek majority and retain only some aspects of their original culture.

An important change in the ethnic makeup of Central Asia occurred in the 1850s to '80s, when the Russian Empire colonized the region and there was a steady influx of "Russians." This population group also included other Slavs, such as Ukrainians and Belarusians, and a significant number of Armenians, Germans, Jews, Poles, Tartars, Greeks, and others. They settled mostly in newly built cities. Although they are estimated as constituting between 5 and 12 percent of the whole population, depending on different interpretations of identity, their contribution to the local culture was considerable.

After Independence, many Russians and Russian-speakers of different ethnicities left the country and changed its ethnic composition once again. Cities such as Tashkent, Andijan, and Ferghana, which had been only 30 to 50 percent Uzbek, are now virtually entirely Uzbek. In 1990, 600,000 Germans lived in Uzbekistan; 95 percent have since left. In 1990, 260,000 Jews lived in Uzbekistan; 90 percent have left.

MAJOR CITIES AND REGIONS
Tashkent
Tashkent is the capital and by far the largest city of Uzbekistan. Its officially registered population was 2.3 million people in the early 2010s, but the actual number is thought to be more than 3 million.

One of the oldest cities in the region, Tashkent was destroyed by Genghis Khan in 1219, but it was later rebuilt and became a prominent strategic center of scholarship, commerce, and trade along the Silk Road. In 1865 it was annexed from the Kokand khanate by Tsarist Russia and became the capital of the Russian colonial enterprise in Central Asia. In Soviet times it witnessed major growth and significant demographic changes. Today the capital of an independent Uzbekistan, Tashkent is its most culturally diverse and modern city, with ethnic Uzbeks as the majority.

EARTHQUAKE

On April 26, 1966, a strong earthquake, measuring 7.5 on the Richter scale, devastated large areas of the old and colonial parts of Tashkent. Over 300,000 residents were left homeless and more than 78,000 adobe houses were destroyed. The Soviet republics and some other countries sent builders and urban planners to help rebuild the city. According to some, Sharaf Rashidov, the First Secretary of the Communist Party of Uzbekistan at the time, took advantage of the disaster to turn Tashkent into a model Soviet city, with wide tree-lined streets, parks, vast squares, fountains, and large residential areas. About 100,000 new homes were built by 1970, and in the following years the city grew even further. Little architectural heritage from Tashkent's ancient history survives. Only a few structures in the old town mark its importance as a strategic city on the Great Silk Road.

Since 1991 the city has changed economically, culturally, and architecturally. New developments have replaced the iconic monuments and edifices of

the Soviet period. Many colonial and early Soviet buildings have been taken down, and others from the late Soviet era have been remodeled. Tashkent's new city center includes banks, modern hotels, business centers, and supermarkets, mostly constructed in a style that involves tinted glass, glossy white walls, and concrete columns, in various proportions.

Samarkand
Samarkand is the oldest and arguably the best-known city in Uzbekistan and in all Central Asia. It is also the most popular tourist destination in the country, with its iconic Registan ensemble, Shahi-Zindah memorial complex, and the Guri-Amir royal mausoleum adorning book covers, billboards, and Uzbek banknotes. With a population of about half a million, it is much smaller than Tashkent and has fewer modern facilities. Although Samarkand seems less affected by Russian culture, the recent restoration has turned most of its historic monuments into sanitized objects of Orientalist admiration.

Yet, beneath the veneer of the hospitality industry there are hidden gems and surprising discoveries to

be made in its old quarters, in the well-preserved but underrated colonial part, in the scenic views from the city's hilltops, and in the country's best wines, beers, unexpectedly good restaurants, and cozy B&Bs.

The old town is still mostly Tajik-speaking, but in recent years almost all the Russian population once living in the green city center has been replaced by Uzbeks and Irani from the city's suburbs, creating an exciting mix of languages on the streets.

Bukhara

Bukhara is more than two thousand years old. It is the most complete example of a medieval city in Central Asia, with over 140 monuments, and an urban environment that has remained mostly intact. Monuments of interest include the tomb of Ismail Samani, a masterpiece

of sophisticated brickwork from the tenth century, and a large number of mausoleums and *madrasas* of the seventeenth. Bukhara's historical city center is on UNESCO's list of World Heritage Sites, which emphasizes that "the real importance of Bukhara lies not in its individual buildings but rather in its overall townscape, demonstrating the high and consistent level of urban planning and architecture that began with the Sheibanid dynasty."

Outside the area of the historical monuments and adobe housing, Bukhara offers little of interest. Like Samarkand, it is located in the Zeravshan Valley, farther into the desert, and can be very hot in summer.

This is a predominantly Tajik-speaking city, but with thousands of tourists visiting its compact old town visitors are greeted in several languages by cheerful children and imperturbable elders alike.

The Ferghana Valley

The Ferghana Valley is Uzbekistan's most densely populated area, home to about one-third of the country's population. It has four important cities: Ferghana, Andijan, Namangan, and the smaller Kokand, which was the capital of a khanate in the nineteenth century.

Surrounded by mountains, the Ferghana Valley is accessible from the rest of Uzbekistan only via the picturesque Kamchik Pass or by air. The natural entrance to the valley now lies in neighboring Tajikistan. The mountains feed a number of small rivers that flow into the valley, making it the greenest region in the country, with large areas of fertile land.

Culturally, the valley is different from other parts of Uzbekistan, as the majority of its population are Uzbeks, although there are small minorities of Tajiks, Kyrgyz, and Kazakhs living on its fringes. The local Uzbeks often regard themselves as the "true Uzbeks," as opposed to those in more multiethnic areas, and are more conservative and religious than the rest.

There are few architectural monuments here to attract visitors, although the nineteenth-century Khan's Palace in Kokand is a remarkable example of Central Asian colonial style. The valley also houses Uzbekistan's largest car factory, assembling the ubiquitous Chevrolet models. The smaller towns of Chust and Margilan are the country's undisputed centers for knife and silk manufacturing respectively.

Khoresm

Khoresm is an ancient oasis region in the north of the country, isolated by the Kyzyl Kum Desert. Located southeast of the Amudarya River Delta, it is also the coldest area in Uzbekistan in winter, although its summers are as hot as everywhere else in the country.

The Uzbeks of Khoresm speak a dialect of the language that sounds closer to Turkmen or Azeri, and the people often call themselves "Khoresmians" to underline their distinctive cultural heritage.

The key attraction is the city of Khiva, the best-preserved "open-air museum" in Uzbekistan, mostly constructed in the eighteenth century, although some older buildings feature prominently in its skyline. There are spectacular ruins of fortresses in the desert, remains of the once mighty Bactrian civilization. The capital of the province is Urgench, a Soviet-style city that has been rebuilt in a modern Uzbek fashion. It has a small international airport that connects it with the rest of Uzbekistan and receives charter flights bringing in tourists who want to bypass Tashkent and plunge straight into the exoticism of the East.

A BRIEF HISTORY

The First Central Asian Kingdoms

The earliest settlers in Central Asia were Indo-Iranian farmers who cultivated wheat and barley. In the first millennium BCE, they started to develop an irrigation system along the rivers of the region and founded the cities of Bukhara and Samarkand, which gradually grew in importance.

By the fifth century BCE, the independent Bactrian, Soghdian, and Tokharian kingdoms dominated the region, having survived frequent onslaughts from Persia. Alexander the Great occupied the area in 328 BCE, bringing it briefly under the control of his empire, which had a lasting cultural influence, especially in what is now southern Uzbekistan.

By the end of the first millennium BCE China had begun to develop its commercial relationships with the West, and the Central Asian cities took advantage of the situation by becoming major trading centers on what was much later called the Great Silk Road. Soghdian merchants traveled as far as Japan in the east and Rome in the west. They dominated the trade along the Silk Road from the second century BCE to the tenth century CE. Because of this trade, Bukhara and Samarkand became extremely prosperous, exceeding Rome and Athens in size.

The wealth of the oases scattered between the Amudarya and Syrdarya Rivers (known as Transoxiana) was a magnet for military incursions from the northern steppes and China. Several local wars were fought between the Soghdian states and the other states in Transoxiana, and the Persians were in endless conflict over the region with the Chinese. The region by now was an important center of intellectual life, culture, and religion. Until the first centuries CE, the dominant religion in was Zoroastrianism, but Buddhism, Manichaeism, and Christianity also attracted many followers.

Turks, Arabs, Mongols, and Tamerlane
The earliest documented Turkic population was a group of nomadic tribes living in Siberia just north of the Great Wall of China, which was built between 206 BCE and 220 CE. The first reference to "Turks" appears in sixth-century Chinese sources. The earliest

evidence of Turkic as a separate linguistic group comes from the so-called Orkhon inscriptions of the early eighth century. In the sixth century the Turks began their westward expansion and formed a loose khaganate that led to perpetual conflict with China.

By the time Central Asia was invaded by the Arabs in 673, the Turkic tribes had already mixed with the local Soghdian population and offered some resistance that lasted until the decisive Battle of Talas in 751, when the Arabs defeated the Chinese and consolidated Transoxiana under Muslim rule.

During the reign of the Abbasid Caliphate in the eighth and ninth centuries, Transoxiana experienced a golden age. Bukhara and Samarkand were centers of culture and art in the Muslim world and, despite strong Arabic influence, the region retained much of its cultural connection with Persia.

In the ninth century, the continued migration of Turks from the north (present-day Kazakhstan) meant that many of these newcomers began to serve in the armies of the states of the region, including the weakening Arab army based in Western Transoxiana and Samarkand and that of the Persian-speaking Samanid Dynasty, based on Bukhara. Gradually some of these soldiers rose to positions of power and eventually established their own states, as other Turkic tribes continued to migrate to Transoxiana. The first of these was the Ghaznavid state, followed by the Karakhanids, Seljuks, and Khoresm shahs, while the whole region continued to be prosperous and rich, maintaining the combination of Persian, Islamic, and Turkic cultures. Everything changed when Genghis Khan and his Mongol armies, which were an amalgam of Mongol and Turkic tribes, invaded Central Asia.

The Mongol subjugation of Central Asia, which took place from 1219 to 1225, quickened the process of Turkification in the region because the invading armies were made up mostly of Turkic horsemen who soon intermixed with the local Turkic- and Persian-speaking population. The Mongol conquest also inflicted large-scale damage on such cities as Bukhara and Samarkand and the whole region of Khoresm. In the early fourteenth century, however, the Mongol empire began to break up as its various tribes and clans competed for influence.

One tribal lord, Timur (Tamerlane), emerged from these scuffles in the 1380s as the main force in Transoxiana and proceeded to conquer Khoresm, Khorasan, Balkh, and the lands near the Caspian Sea, and to dominate the rest of Central Asia, Iran, Asia Minor, India, and the Caucasus. Timur became the most powerful ruler in the Muslim world after crushing the Mamluks of Egypt and Syria, the emerging Ottoman Empire, and the weakening Delhi Sultanate. He also attacked Russia, before he died during an invasion of China in 1405.

Timur's legacy is highly controversial. While Central Asia blossomed under his reign, other places including Baghdad, Damascus, Delhi, and many other great Asian cities were sacked and demolished and their populations slaughtered. In any case, Timur was the last great nomadic warrior, who brought about the last flowering of Transoxiana by gathering in Samarkand, his capital, artisans and scholars from the lands he had conquered. He patronized scientists and artists, and his grandson Ulugbek was one of the world's first great astronomers. It was during the Timurid dynasty that Turkic, in the form of the Chaghatai dialect, became a literary language, later adopted by a new wave of invaders from the north.

Uzbek Rule

The Uzbeks owe their name to a group of Turkic–Mongol nomadic tribes who converted to Islam in the fourteenth century in southern Siberia.

In the early fifteenth century, Abu al-Khayr Khan, a descendant of Genghis Khan, led them south to the steppe and semidesert north of the Syrdarya River. By 1510, under Muhammad Shaybani Khan, they had occupied the fertile land of modern Uzbekistan. The Uzbeks ousted Timur's heirs from Samarkand and Herat (now in northwestern Afghanistan) and established new city-states. The most powerful of these was the khanate of Bukhara, which controlled the whole area between the Amudarya and the Syrdarya, as well as the region of Tashkent, the fertile Ferghana Valley, and northern Afghanistan. The second Uzbek state, the khanate of Khiva, was established in the oasis of Khoresm in 1512. Settling down, the Uzbeks exchanged their nomadic lifestyle for urban life and agriculture.

The first century of Uzbek rule was marked by thriving culture and the arts, but the Shaybanid dynasty gradually slipped into decline, hastened by the end of the Silk Road trade after the opening up of the sea route to the east. In 1749 invaders from Iran took over Bukhara and Khiva, breaking up the weakened states. What followed was the Emirate of Bukhara, which included Samarkand, and the khanates of Khiva and Kokand, all involved in perpetual internecine wars until the Russians arrived.

Russian Turkestan

Tsarist Russia became interested in Central Asia in the eighteenth century. Concerned that the British might break through from India and get there first, it was also motivated by anger over the plight of Russians captured and enslaved by local tribesmen; by the desire to control trade in the region; and by the wish to establish a secure supply of cotton. Finally, Russia wanted to prove its worth as an Empire that held its own portion of the east. After a couple of unsuccessful attempts, the Russians

invaded the emirate of Bukhara in 1868, and brutally conquered the khanate of Khiva in 1873. Both were made protectorates and retained a quasi-independent status. In 1876, Kokand was annexed and made part of the Russian province of Turkestan, which soon saw the arrival of Russian settlers.

During the first decades of Russian rule, the daily life of the Central Asians remained almost unchanged. The Russians substantially increased cotton production, but otherwise they interfered little with the natives. They built new towns next to cities such as Tashkent, Samarkand, Namangan, and Andijan, but did not mix much with the local population.

As time went on, Russian rule did bring about important social and economic changes for many Uzbeks; a new, educated middle class developed, and rural areas were increasingly affected by the emphasis on cotton production. In the late nineteenth century the newly built Transcaspian Railway brought greater numbers of Russians into the region.

In the 1910s the Jadid reform movement, led by local intellectuals inspired by the Turkish and Caucasian models, sought to establish a new national community of Muslims in the region that was free both of conservative Islamic parochialism and of colonial Russian rule. They helped create a growing awareness among people of their national identities.

Soviet Uzbekistan

Hopes for either national autonomy or complete independence were kindled by an armed uprising against the Tsarist conscription law in 1916 and by the following two Russian Revolutions in 1917; but by 1921 it became clear that the Soviet regime had reunited the collapsed Russian Empire and that some

new states were about to emerge. Some Jadidists and other loosely connected groups began what was called the Basmachi Revolt against Soviet rule, which lasted for more than a decade, while the majority of Jadidists, including their leaders, threw in their lot with the Soviets.

In 1924 Soviet planners, local authorities, and Central Asian intellectuals determined the borders of the new Soviet Socialist Republics of Uzbekistan and Karakalpakstan based on the dominant ethnic groups. In 1929, Tajikistan was split off from the south of Uzbekistan, causing lasting friction between the Uzbeks, who saw Tajiks as Persianized Uzbeks, and the Tajiks, who were unhappy that the predominantly Tajik-speaking cities of Bukhara and Samarkand were given to the Uzbeks, whom the Tajiks saw as

Turkic invaders from the north. Karakalpakstan was transferred to Uzbekistan in 1936 as an autonomous republic. By the beginning of the Second Word War, the Soviet nationality-building program was firmly on course, and after the war the Soviet leaders managed to integrate loose ethnic groups and their subcultures into what would become the Uzbek national culture.

In the post-Stalin period more Uzbeks began to join the Communist Party of

Uzbekistan and to assume positions in government, albeit on terms set out in Moscow. Local Russians were either gradually relegated to secondary roles, such as deputies of first secretaries, directors, chairpersons, and other top posts then occupied by Uzbeks, or remained highly respected but essentially powerless specialists providing technical expertise at different levels. As Uzbeks started gaining leading positions in society, they also began establishing informal networks based on regional and family connections and personal allegiances. These connections permeated the official structures and provided different kinds of support that the new generation of leaders were keen to use to their own benefit.

Independence

The liberalizing agenda of *perestroika* (reconstruction) launched by Soviet leader Mikhail Gorbachev in 1985 brought about social changes that included new opportunities to express dissent, as well as mounting economic challenges. The Uzbeks expressed their grievances over the cotton monoculture, economic stagnation, Russian cultural domination, restriction of religious and traditional life, and the lack of investment in industrial development to provide more job opportunities. Following bloody ethnic clashes in the Ferghana Valley between Uzbeks, Kyrgyz, and Meskhetian Turks (an ethnic subgroup deported from Georgia in 1944) in 1989 and 1990, Uzbek identity became more assertive; then after the failure of the reactionary coup against Mikhail Gorbachev in August 1991, Uzbekistan declared its independence from the USSR on September 1, 1991.

UZBEKISTAN TODAY

Though moving away from Communism, the late President Islam Karimov, who had been the First Secretary of the Communist Party in Uzbekistan, managed to maintain strict control over the independent state. In many respects, of all the ex-USSR countries, Uzbekistan is the one that most resembles the Soviet Union, in both public and private sectors. Little, if any, political opposition, a vast bureaucratic class supported by a massive police force, and a number of human rights and civil restrictions ensured the kind of political stability that enabled Uzbekistan to come through several crises shaken but intact. The economic and demographic situation forced many young people, especially from rural areas, to emigrate to countries such as Russia, Kazakhstan, and Korea in search of better jobs. This may have reduced potential social tension, as it remains difficult for less-qualified workers to find a well-paid job, especially in the overpopulated villages.

At the same time, relatively low living costs, plentiful locally produced food supplies, and significant financial resources enabled the government to address some of the problems burdening the country. There has been improvement in the transportation network, rural housing, the provision of education facilities, the streamlining of government services, and diversification of the economy.

Overall, Uzbekistan today is a paradoxical country—populated by relaxed and hospitable people, but governed by a strict bureaucratic regime. In areas such as personal freedom, business attractiveness, and transparency there is a lot to be desired.

GOVERNMENT AND POLITICS

The Republic of Uzbekistan is a presidential constitutional republic. The president is both head of state and de facto head of government. Legislative power is vested in the two chambers of the Supreme Assembly (Oliy Majlis): the Senate, which has 100 members, and the Legislative Chamber, with 150. The Judiciary is composed of the Supreme Court, the Constitutional Court, and the Higher Economic Court.

The president is elected by popular vote for a five-year term in elections that have been the subject of international criticism. The president appoints the prime minister and other ministers. In fact, the executive branch holds almost all the power; the powers of the judiciary and the legislature are relatively limited. The president selects and replaces provincial governors (*hokims*). The power of the Service of National Security and, to a lesser extent, the Ministry of Internal Affairs is as strong as ever. There are several political parties, but none is truly oppositional. They offer a limited choice of policies within the narrow confines of mainstream Uzbek politics.

THE ECONOMY

Uzbekistan has rich reserves of gold, oil, natural gas, coal, silver, and copper—a potential base for economic development— but it still has a mostly agricultural economy. Much of its industrial production is in one way or another linked to agriculture. The country was the principal source of cotton for the textile industry in the Soviet Union. Today it is the world's fifth-largest cotton producer and second-largest cotton exporter. Only part of the cotton and silk production is processed locally.

Although the country remains a supplier of raw material goods for downstream manufacturing elsewhere in the world, in recent years both government-owned and private businesses have invested heavily in local processing and manufacture of textiles.

Uzbekistan's centrally planned economy has few privatized sectors. Most production and employment remain in the state sector, and most health, education, and welfare services are provided by the government. The steps taken toward developing a free market economy have been less radical than in other post-Soviet states.

RELATIONS WITH THE WORLD

Uzbekistan's foreign policy over the years has been strategically consistent but tactically rather fragmented and volatile. A member of the Commonwealth of Independent States, it retains close links with almost all the ex-Soviet republics, in particular Russia, but it is wary of Russian neo-colonial ambitions and is not a member of the Russian-led Eurasian Economic Union and the Collective Security Treaty Organization.

There are a number of unresolved issues with its neighbors—the perceived Islamist threat from Afghanistan and Tajikistan, water resource and border disputes with Kyrgyzstan and Tajikistan, and economic competition with Kazakhstan—but by and large it is able to maintain good relations with them.

Relations with the outside world have seen highs and lows, mostly due to criticism of the human rights situation by the West and the promotion of orthodox Islam by certain Middle Eastern countries. There are good working relationships with the powerful trio of Korea, Japan, and China, and the huge Chinese project of the New Great Silk Road is set to seriously influence its economic development in the future.

VALUES & ATTITUDES

NATIONALITY AND ETHNICITY

In Uzbekistan people tend to take their ethnic identity very seriously, and few things would offend them more than being mistaken for someone else. The question "Are you Russian?" may provoke the emotional answer "Of course not! I'm Armenian (or Uzbek, Tajik, Tartar)." On the other hand, such heavy emphasis on ethnicity has made the people of Uzbekistan more aware of and accommodating to people of other ethnic origins. As in most post-Soviet countries, "nationality" is not a synonym for citizenship but a reference to ethnicity. Although the current nationalities were constructed in the 1920s during the Soviet nationality-building program, the predominant perception of nationality in Uzbekistan is "primordialist"—the Uzbeks, Kazakhs, Tajiks, Russians, and so on are seen as essentially different peoples with their individual cultures, languages, and minds rooted in deep history and certain genetic features.

In the USSR, a person's nationality was shown in his or her passport, and one could choose either the father's or the mother's nationality at the age of sixteen if the marriage was considered "mixed," for example between an ethnic Uzbek and an ethnic Armenian. Most children chose their father's nationality. If the nationality of a parent was seen as problematic (Jewish, Crimean Tartar, German), the more "neutral" nationality of the other parent (such as Russian, Uzbek, Ukrainian) would be chosen. Over the seventy years of Soviet history the government's policy toward different nationalities fluctuated from internationalism to Russian chauvinism to policies resembling affirmative action.

In Uzbekistan, many believe that in the 1920s a large part of the local population who should have been registered as Tajiks or Kazakhs were recorded instead as Uzbeks, thereby giving the latter an overwhelming majority in the republic. After independence many children from mixed families were also recorded as Uzbeks, apparently to make their life in the country easier. Uzbekistan is one of several post-Soviet countries where ethnicity is still recorded in a person's passport, although not on the international English-language page.

In reality, the boundaries between local nationalities and even larger ethnic groups are

somewhat blurred, while differences within the same
nationality can be quite visible. In Samarkand, local
Uzbeks and Tajiks are essentially the same people
speaking different languages as their mother tongue
(with both groups speaking the other's as the second
language). The ethnically homogeneous population
of the Ferghana Valley, with fewer national
minorities living among the Uzbeks, is often
regarded as the only "true" and "pure" Uzbek. For
the Uzbeks of Khoresm, in the north of the country,
their regional identity seems even more important
than nationality. They often call themselves and
their language "Khoresmian." On the other hand,
Tashkent is a melting pot of different nationalities
and ethnicities.

The only obvious dividing line can be drawn
between the descendants of those who had lived in
Central Asia before the 1860s and the descendants
of "Russians" who had colonized the region by the
late nineteenth century. To recognize the diversity
of the latter group, its members are often referred
to as "the Europeans," and consequently the sign
"National and European Cuisine" displayed by a café
would mean that it offers a range of Russian as well
as local dishes.

Further divisions can be seen between the Uzbeks
and their once nomadic Kazakh, Karakalpak, and
Kyrgyz neighbors, and between the Uzbeks and the
Tajiks. Despite some friction between these groups,
they have generally managed to maintain friendly
relations. Some communities, especially in the cities,
are truly and encouragingly multicultural. People are
very aware of others' different ethnicities, and this
awareness provides a rich cultural background for

banter and jokes that would be considered risky or even racist in more politically correct cultures.

To avoid complications, in this book the term "Uzbek" signifies the ethnic majority, which may also include representatives of other Central Asian nationalities if not stated otherwise. The term "Russians" refers to the heterogeneous post-1860s minority, and where there is a need to identify a particular group or nationality (such as Germans or Tartars), they are specifically mentioned as such.

THE URBAN AND RURAL DIVIDE

Over 60 percent of the population of the country is rural, and predominantly Uzbek. Most country folk have a conservative outlook, and until recently rarely traveled abroad or even across Uzbekistan. City people are usually more liberal and have greater exposure to the world. Although Uzbeks also form the majority

of the urban population, the presence of other nationalities in cities and the Russian/Soviet origin of modern urban life make the town and country divide even more noticeable. Most of the present-day cities of Uzbekistan are ancient, and some are among the oldest in the world. However, by the time of the Russian invasion they had gone into decline, and the Russians built colonial settlements next to old towns that were administered separately until the Soviets launched an ambitious urbanization program that affected both the colonizer and the colonized. Although it was meant to liberate the latter and to erase this very divide, in practice it had the effect of imposing the Russian view of industrial utopia on the local population, which was encouraged to abandon their "backward" way of life in favor of "progressive" Socialist culture.

As a result, by the time of independence the population of some cities, such as Tashkent, Navoi, or Ferghana was predominantly Russian, and the rest were Russian-speaking Uzbeks who had by and large adopted the Soviet urban lifestyle. The mass emigration of the Russians in the 1990s and early 2000s has dramatically changed the ethnic composition of the urban population, but cultural changes in the cities were never as significant. The government of Uzbekistan has continued the Soviet modernist agenda, which has made cities even more attractive to the rural population who moved in to replace the Russians only to find the need to adapt to the city life a challenge.

Consequently, in the 2010s the government attempted to restrict migration from the villages and provinces to the cities and the capital, first by making registration in cities more difficult and then by investing in the rural infrastructure. Although the difference in lifestyle in villages and cities remains as great as ever, it would be a gross simplification to assume that "urban" always means "liberal" and "rural" conservative. It could well be the other way around. Also, promotional materials tend to exoticize Uzbekistan, emphasizing the traditional and distinctive side of life in the country that's rarely seen in larger cities, especially Tashkent.

THE FAMILY
The Traditional Family

The family is the core of Uzbek society, and family values are nearly universally accepted as given by all classes of the society. A typical Uzbek family is patriarchal, but this gender bias, so obvious to a foreign visitor, is rarely questioned even by women. The traditional Uzbek family is extended, with several generations living around the same courtyard in different sections of a large house. With five or six children in one family and lots of relatives living in the same or nearby premises, an Uzbek household is a flexible and helpful organizational unit, well integrated in a settled and socially stable community. An important principle of family (and of society's) organization is the hierarchy of age. Old people are respected, treated with deference, listened to, obeyed, and looked after. It is unthinkable for children to allow their parents to end their lives in an old people's home; it is the duty of the younger children to stay with and care for their parents.

Traditionally, Uzbek women are not supposed to work. Although this attitude is often attributed to Islam, in reality it stems from the traditional patriarchal structure of the whole society. In a large family, women simply have no time to do anything apart from their household duties. Also, a woman who works outside the home may be seen as an indication of her husband's inability to provide her with the necessary means or to install the appropriate hierarchical order. Such traditional families are typical in ethnically homogeneous villages and small towns, but in large cities the situation is more complex.

The Modern Family

Urban communities are strongly influenced by Russian and other cultures, and retain only some features of the traditional family structure. Although Uzbeks typically prefer to live in their own house with a courtyard, in large cities they usually have to live in apartments built in the second half of the twentieth century in a communal environment very different from the quiet and settled rural life. Such families have fewer children, usually one or two, and normally both parents work. Everyday concerns, such as driving children to school, paying community bills, shopping in a bazaar or supermarket, and visiting relatives on holidays, are shared by urban families of all nationalities. Depending on social class, people retain more or less of their traditional culture, which becomes more evident at family events or when receiving guests.

HOSPITALITY

Hospitality is a core value in Uzbekistan. It reflects people's respect for their guests, and also gives a family an opportunity to reassert its social status in the community. Receiving visitors and visiting other families is a long and well-established ritual, with clearly assigned roles for hosts and guests. The more traditional a family is, the more it adheres to the rules of hospitality. Modern families are more relaxed, but the principle remains the same: guests are treated with respect, a lot of attention, a lot of food, and somewhat surprisingly little regard for their individual tastes and preferences.

Foreign visitors are usually embarrassed by being treated as guests of honor, and by the sheer quantity of food and drink offered to them and try to resist, usually in vain. It is important to remember, however, that token resistance is all right but public rejection of an offering is considered impolite and causes huge embarrassment for the hosts. If you *really* do not drink vodka, or are a vegetarian, it is advisable to inform the hosts about it in advance, to spare them public humiliation, and offer a plausible explanation, such as medical or religious considerations, that don't imply your rejection of their tradition. If you are offered a slice of horse sausage, don't reply, "No, I won't eat it. At home, we don't eat friends." Think of something more tactful. Otherwise, relax and enjoy the treatment!

COMMUNITY

The traditional community unit in Uzbekistan is known as the *mahalla*—a neighborhood from several to several dozen households. The Uzbek *mahalla* has a long history and is the focal point for family and religious holidays. As a rule, each community has its own small mosque, teahouse, and bazaar. In the Soviet period, mosques were converted into libraries or local administrative units. After Independence the *mahalla* was institutionalized but lost most of its democratic power as an independent, self-governing body. Now it performs local administrative functions on behalf of the government as a territorial association of families fostering cooperation and mutual assistance.

Neighbors are the second-most important people for Uzbeks after their family. Traditionally, you spend all your life in the same community, growing up with the same people and sharing with them your food, joys, and sorrows. Such communal organization implies establishment of close relations with all the neighbors, regularly reinforced by reciprocal visits, exchanges of gifts on certain occasions, and communal charity work known as *hashar*.

This flexible and resilient communal network requires compliance with the rules established in the neighborhood, ensured by families who voluntarily give up certain rights to privacy in exchange for communal support. If you wear the same clothes as everyone else, drive the same kind of car, participate in all the traditional events, respect your neighbors, obey your parents, and don't mix with people considered strange, you can be sure that when you need to borrow some rice, or a ladder, or when you need someone to look after your son while you are at work, your neighbors will be there to help you.

This collectivist lifestyle strongly contrasts with the individualism of the more socially mobile and self-sufficient urban Russians. In the larger cities, especially in new residential areas with apartment blocks, the traditional *mahalla* structure has merged with the Soviet-style administration and a certain cultural compromise has been reached. The social openness of the Uzbeks has also greatly influenced the local Russians, who often find it difficult to adapt to the more cold and reserved attitudes between neighbors when they move to Russia proper.

SECULARISM AND RELIGION

Religion plays an ambivalent role in Uzbek society. There are sixteen religious groups in Uzbekistan, and although Islam is recognized as the main faith (according to a US State Department release in 2009, 90 percent of the population are Muslims, mostly Sunni of the Khanafite branch), it is seen and promoted as part of traditional culture and not as a world religion. Therefore, Uzbekistan is a secular state, not a Muslim state as such. All forms of religious fundamentalism and radicalism are prohibited.

The government of Uzbekistan has always been acutely aware of the threat of Islamism in the region, especially from neighboring Afghanistan and Tajikistan, as they went through civil wars involving religious extremism. It chose a hard-line approach that was strongly criticized in the West, although this criticism has considerably softened as the more balanced strategies of dealing with extreme Islamism have by and large failed to deliver the desired result.

The firm place of religion in culture, coupled with strict government control, gives religion in Uzbekistan a strong secular flavor, underpinned by the similar attitude to religious practices in Soviet times. Paradoxically, it has also enabled the local variety of Islam to retain many pre-Islamic features that would make an orthodox Sunni wince, including magical practices and talismans, superstitions, the use of fire and water in some rituals, and the worshiping of holy places and the dead. Although the Sufi schools of old are not common today, they have helped to nurture a relaxed and eclectic attitude to Islam. The embracing of religion is therefore more of a cultural statement than a matter of conviction or belief. The attitude to religion today is reverential but relaxed, and nobody cares what you actually believe as long as you conform generally and take part in all the communal religious ceremonies.

In general, the most conservative form of Islam is practiced in the Ferghana Valley, while in Tashkent it has become fashionable to fast during the holy month of Ramadan; in other cities Islamic practices are visible only in mosques and during family religious ceremonies. Very few people read Arabic, and even the mullahs usually recite prayers in Uzbek or Tajik, framed by some formulaic memorized quotations from the Quran.

Russian Orthodox Christianity is the second-largest religion in the country. According to the same US State Department release, about 5 percent of the population are Orthodox Christians. However, as with the statistical data about Muslims, this figure includes those who feel culturally affiliated with Orthodox Christianity, mostly the Slavonic population and some Tartars, Georgians, and Armenians. The number of devout churchgoers is much smaller. To many, Christianity is just a visible symbol of their Russian identity. Orthodox Christians gather in large numbers in local churches to celebrate Easter, and many exchange Easter eggs the next day.

There are smaller communities of Catholics, Lutherans, Baptists, members of the Armenian Apostolic Church, and other denominations. In general, Uzbek society tolerates Christian groups as long as they do not attempt to win converts among ethnic Uzbeks; the law prohibits or severely restricts activities such as proselytizing, importing, and disseminating religious literature, and offering private religious instruction.

There used to be about 95,000 Jews in Uzbekistan, but by the 2010s their number had shrunk to a mere 5,000. All of these are automatically counted as followers of Judaism, but the number of actual believers is unknown. The followers of such religions and cults as Jehovah's Witnesses, the Hare Krishna movement, Paganism, and Baha'i enjoy comparatively less freedom of worship compared to the representatives of larger denominations.

ATTITUDES TOWARD EDUCATION

One of the defining features of Uzbekistan (and other post-Soviet states) that distinguishes it from its southern neighbors is its literacy rate of nearly 98 percent. Compulsory secondary education, a legacy of the Soviet Union, has helped to flatten the social structure and has given, at least in theory, an equal opportunity to all citizens to pursue higher education.

The traditional Uzbek attitude to education is that of profound respect, and teachers of all kinds and levels are treated with marked deference. Formal education is greatly valued, especially higher education, at least partly due to the higher social status ascribed to a person with a university degree. This is true for all social classes, but in different ways. For the rural population, higher education is a way to secure a better job, especially in a city, and move up the social ladder. For the middle classes it is an opportunity to reinforce and enhance their status and to form new social, family, and power alliances. Members of the upper classes send their children to prestigious local or foreign universities as a means of reaching a nationally or internationally recognized status, crucial for their aspiration to accrue power. The primary objectives of acquiring an education— the development of new skills and professional competency—are often relegated to secondary importance, especially in traditional communities.

There is a lot of social pressure on young people to get a "proper" higher education to fit them for the modern world. However, many university students develop two separate attitudes toward their future professional and social development. On one hand they would like to become competent, successful, and autonomous professionals of an international caliber, but on the other they persist in seeing critical thinking as a form of disobedience, individual opinion as an expression of disrespect, and "why" questions as undermining traditional values. These conflicting agendas are held by different social groups and institutions to a varying degree, in an ethnically and socially diverse student population.

WORK ETHIC

As with all other aspects of life in Uzbekistan, the attitude to work is a curious mix of Soviet, Central Asian, and global influences, and much will depend on the context. Different rules apply when a man is building a house for his family, or goes to his routine job in a local town council, or is developing a customer survey for a cell phone company.

Generally speaking, the Uzbeks are hardworking and driven by long-term goals when they work for themselves. Tradition and specific local conditions play an important role in how they work. They often start very early and finish late, but tend to have a long lunch. The pace of work is not particularly fast, and the methods they use are not modern or the most efficient, but people usually know what they are doing and can concentrate on their job for a long time. Decisions are often based on intuition and established practice, which is rarely questioned, making the development of common ground in a team and mutual understanding easy. Relationships are more important than formal structures, and this allows space for bargaining and flexibility. Reciprocity and social cohesion are the key principles of the Uzbek work ethic, which can lead both to an easy and informal working environment and to corruption.

The formal structure in Uzbek businesses, especially in government bodies, tends to be bureaucratic and top heavy. The system is overregulated by many contradictory rules and control mechanisms, and even routine decisions to be made at the top level. However, once a rapport is established, things move ahead much more smoothly. Power relations at work are hierarchical and spread beyond the workplace into other aspects of public and social life.

The work ethic of both private businesses and international organizations functioning in Uzbekistan is strongly influenced by these factors, and the result is an amalgam of personal relationships, bureaucracy, and the impersonal efficiency of the modern global business machine.

THE VALUE OF MONEY

People's attitude to money may seem paradoxical to an outsider. As the country is not rich by international standards, the issue of personal wealth is extremely important in society. Wealth is often displayed ostentatiously and social status can be determined by a person's ability to make money in a certain position of power. The acquiring of higher social status becomes an overarching life objective for many; however, in everyday life people prefer to set short-term goals in a fluid and often unpredictable business environment. That is not to say that long-term planning is impossible, but that it is often seen as a series of repetitive opportunistic tactical deals.

On the other hand, Uzbeks can be extremely generous, even lavish, with their money. In a traditional context, a lot of money is allocated to different forms of social cohesion, such as giving gifts or receiving visitors. The need for good personal relationships often trumps financial gain. This results in the prodigal hospitality that so often baffles foreign visitors, and in various charitable donations with religious undertones (such as donating money to a poor neighbor on the occasion of his son's ritual circumcision).

Foreign visitors, as a rule, are seen socially as guests of honor and are treated as such. However, when the gears are switched from a social to a business context, the driving factors behind the interaction also change, determining people's attitude to money in that particular situation.

ATTITUDES TOWARD AUTHORITY

Uzbek society is highly hierarchical, and authority is respected, obeyed, and desired. The vertical axis of power is particularly strong in government institutions; it is partly offset in traditional businesses by the need for social harmony, and in private and international companies by the global preference for flatter power structures. A good manager is seen as strong and assertive, but committed and caring. Things are usually managed by top-down decisions and orders, not through involvement and motivation, although personal management styles may vary. Power relationships in a typical Uzbek organization are those of hierarchical subordination, and imply a firm working discipline and obedience that may also hamper the ability of low-level managers to solve issues without referring to their superiors.

Apart from formal power relationships, Uzbek society depends strongly on informal social networks that soften the bureaucratic rigidity of the official structures and can speed up decision making at different levels. These networks are built around people occupying various posts in education, health care, the police, administrative bodies, or business, linked through family, friendship, communal, and other connections. Westerners may view such informal networks as corrupt or nepotistic, but this would be to ignore their great contribution to social harmony and cohesion, so important for Uzbek culture, and overlook the flexibility they give to an otherwise rigid public system.

RESPECT FOR AGE

In the Uzbek family, older members are respected and treated with great deference by younger ones. Young girls and boys must speak politely not only to their parents and grandparents but to everyone above their

age. This attitude is reflected in both the Uzbek and the Russian languages. There are no such generic words as "brother" and "sister" in Uzbek. Instead, it has separate words for older brother (*aka*) and younger brother (*uka*), older (*opa*) and younger (*singil*) sister. These words are also used outside the family context to establish age and power relations between speakers or to indicate particular levels of respect in a way that resembles the Japanese use of -*san*: Alisher-*aka*, Matluba-*opa*, or simply *opa-jon* (literally, *dear elder sister*, a rough equivalent of "Ma'am"). In a formal context Uzbeks often use the Russian form of addressing an elder, by using the first name and the patronymic, as in Alisher Juraevich (see pages 71–3).

Whereas in modern English the second person is treated as plural ("you are") and is therefore neutral in tone, in Uzbek the plural form of you (*siz*) is the sign of respect used by strangers and is the way to address your parents and other older family members. The second person singular (*san*) is used when addressing children or close friends, and is otherwise considered rude. In Russian, the rules are similar but more relaxed, and children usually call their friends and parents *tee* (singular), while *vee* (plural) is reserved for strangers and elders.

Given the traditional Uzbek respect for elders, coupled with the overall respect for power, you might think that at work the oldest people wield near absolute authority; this is not always the case. The elderly are more likely to be at the top in places where their power or expertise is rarely questioned, such as in their own private businesses, or in traditional craft workshops where they are held in a high esteem as masters by their students. In more fluid types of organization, although older employees are certainly respected and even revered for their experience, they seldom occupy top positions.

Many people complain that in modern society, especially in the cities, the traditional attitudes to older people have faded, but in any case, they can still be summed up in one word: respect.

ATTITUDES TOWARD WOMEN

Attitudes toward women vary, depending on the context, from liberal to outright sexist, but they almost always correspond to the expectations of a particular community. Traditional Uzbek women are not supposed to work, and their main responsibility is to stay at home and look after the children and other relatives. This way of life, developed over centuries, was strongly influenced by Islamic norms regulating gender relationships. However, the years of emancipation under the Soviets changed social attitudes, especially in the cities, where many families adopted some of the more liberal attitudes toward women of the Russian and other European communities.

In Uzbekistan, as well as in other countries of Central Asia, discrimination against women is prohibited, and in public life women enjoy greater freedom than in most Muslim majority countries. They can work in any position, occupy any post, and receive any kind of education. However, in many contexts, the traditional attitude toward women affects their public standing, and there is a lot of adjustment from one situation to another.

A female boss can be compared to a strict mother-in-law who runs the household and supervises the activities of her younger relatives. In the office she may seem cold, bureaucratic, and formidable, enjoying the somewhat servile attitudes of her subordinates, but in a social setting the same woman may turn into a flamboyant, hospitable, and generous hostess, anxious to make all others feel welcome.

The Traditional Woman
To an outsider, a woman's life in a traditional context may seem tough. In a conservative Uzbek family, a

girl's behavior is strictly controlled by her parents. They try to arrange a marriage for her at a relatively early age, after which she is subordinated to her husband and, very importantly, to her mother-in-law. Many young students drop out of higher education to get married, and there is a lot of social pressure to produce a child in the first year of marriage.

Today, however, even in villages it is acceptable for a woman to work in a position that might be seen as an extension of her usual family duties: as a teacher, nurse, seamstress, cook, cleaner, and so on. She is expected to come home directly after work to prepare dinner for the family, and risks her reputation if she is seen walking alone in the evening. Women usually pay social visits to other families with their husbands, but sit separately from men. They attend special women's parties and events without men.

Traditional women usually wear traditional costume, or at least long dresses and skirts, and have long hair, especially in the more traditional areas. Trousers have become more common in recent years as a more practical kind of dress and are generally accepted, unlike miniskirts or shorts.

Yet the impression of the almost complete subjugation of women is misleading. As an oft-quoted Uzbek proverb goes, "The husband may be the head of a family, but the wife is the neck, which determines the direction where head will look." Women are responsible for their household and can shape it according to their taste; they also exercise almost complete control over the way their children are raised. If young women have their husbands imposed on them, in compensation they can bring up their sons according to their own ideals, and this power of a mother has a lasting influence on young Uzbek men. The women are the true keepers of tradition, morals, and style in a family, and their role, even in the most conservative families, should not be underestimated.

Modern Women

Gender relations in the cities are extremely complex.
They combine some of the traditional attitudes
described above with the attributes of modern global
society, such as equal education and employment

rights, secular
public life, and
exposure to
different cultural
and behavioral
options. It is
worth noting
that although
Russian attitudes
to women have
been influential
in shaping
urban gender
relationships,
they have been
affected in turn by local conditions, resulting in an
fascinating mix of attitudes and behaviors.

The modern urban Uzbek woman is a mistress of
role play. Ideally, she takes advantage of the best that
the local cultures can offer to women while trying
to avoid their less attractive features. She wants to be
valued as an independent person, capable of making
her own decisions, yet she does not quite embrace
feminist self-sufficiency; she wants her femininity to
be recognized and admired, but does not want to be
a subservient housewife. However, it is her ability to
adapt to a particular social context that makes her so
flexible: even the most emancipated woman will be a
caring mother and a hospitable host.

In general, women rarely live alone, and if they do it may raise some questions in the neighborhood. Russian and, especially, foreign women are usually less restricted by Uzbek cultural codes, but they are not entirely free from the traditionalist judgment, either. Nobody will mind if a foreign woman smokes, wears trousers, or socializes with men, but being out alone in the evening and excessive drinking may be frowned upon by some and seen as an invitation by others.

For women visiting Uzbekistan, the rule of thumb is simple common sense. Nobody expects you to wear traditional clothes and behave like an obedient housewife from a distant village, but it's prudent to be culturally sensitive, and to be aware of how some forms of behavior may be interpreted.

ATTITUDES TOWARD HOMOSEXUALITY

Uzbekistan is one of the few countries in the world where male homosexuality is a criminal offence, but there are no documented cases of anybody having been convicted for it. By modern international standards, Uzbekistan can be regarded a homophobic country, but the reality is less straightforward. As recently as the early twentieth century there were communities of teenage boys (*bacha*) who were trained to dance, sing, and otherwise entertain guests, and the tradition is not entirely forgotten. Another factor softening public attitudes has been the traditional unavailability of any sexual activity with girls, pushing some boys into experimentation. In other words, it is not homosexuality itself that most people find objectionable, but an overt display of it in public. Interestingly, female homosexuality is neither punishable by law nor seen as particularly offensive, although the idea of a lesbian or gay family will still be shocking to most.

Traveling around with a partner of the same gender is fine as long as your appearance and your relationship with the partner generally fall within culturally conservative norms of friendship.

ATTITUDES TOWARD TIME

As in other aspects of public life in Uzbekistan, attitudes toward time differ greatly, depending on the context. In general, people tend to have a lot of free time, and the pace of life is slow and relaxed. In many families it is common to sit for several hours in the evening, just chatting, watching TV, and drinking tea. People spend some time on social rituals when meeting relatives and friends or receiving guests, and may be offended when such readiness to spend time together is not reciprocated. Social gatherings are there to be enjoyed, and any haste is considered impolite, therefore turning up even an hour late for a large event with many guests is fine. When an event is held in a restaurant, being on time is more important. However, it is still common to drop by at somebody's house unannounced and hang out for hours. Typically, women are expected to be late, even for a date.

Although generally speaking punctuality is not seen as important in everyday life, in administrative, business, and educational institutions employees and students are expected to arrive on time. This rule is more relaxed for figures of authority, and in many administrative bodies people often have to wait for senior officials for a long time.

There is a marked difference between government and private or international institutions in their approaches to time management. Administrative bodies have inherited from the Soviet period a set of attitudes that can be summarized as follows. First, there is a direct link between a person's punctuality and his or her rank. Senior officials may often be late for meetings, but junior employees often cannot go home before their boss. Second, officials are almost always "very busy," they "have a lot of urgent work," and "no time." It is common for administrative institutions to work until late. Not only does this raise their self-importance but it is also more often than not a consequence of inefficient time management in a highly hierarchical bureaucratic structure, where some key decisions are taken only by senior managers. This bureaucratic inefficiency means that things move slowly, deadlines are regularly missed, and there are always many matters to deal with urgently. Although the government has taken steps to streamline bureaucracy—such as introducing a range of online services—on average, time management in administrative institutions, especially at lower levels, leaves much to be desired.

Time management in private companies and international organizations is strongly influenced by global business culture and is therefore more efficient. The same can be said about most of the new elements of the country's infrastructure, such as fast trains and intercity flights, while the older and more provincial service providers are not marked by the same degree of punctuality. The trains and airplanes are generally on time, but most city buses, underground trains, and intercity coaches do not follow a strict timetable.

In general, the farther you are from the capital, the city center, and modern institutions, the more relaxed the attitude toward time. There is little you can do about it, but it is important to know what to expect.

STATUS

The form and degree of the respect given someone is closely linked to their position in Uzbek society. Traditionally, status in Uzbekistan was ascribed rather than achieved, but with the arrival of the modern state, with its social mobility and private capital, the role of achieved status has grown in importance. The key indicator of a person's status is proximity to power. However, this power is "context dependent," that is, not restricted to an individual, but usually spread across a community of family, friends, schoolmates, and other contacts.

Uzbek society is diffuse; any status that a person has at work will be recognized socially, and vice versa. In a communal society, it means that everyone is a member of several overlapping networks where status is formally and informally shared and exchanged. A wealthy businessman, a distinguished professor, or the son of a popular artist possesses a certain status that he carries around in society. In the modern context, even if this status is achieved, it is converted into a communal commodity—so the family or friends of the son of a famous parent can all bask in the connection.

The traditional categories of ascribed status—such as class, kin, ethnicity, or birthplace—create powerful social bonds and serve as a ground for the formation of so-called "clans," usually defined in broad geographical terms (the Tashkent clan, the Samarkand clan, and so on). In the 1990s, these clans underpinned even the formal power structure within the country, but by now they have evolved into a more flexible and socially open system.

The Russian-speaking community is generally more meritocratic and socially mobile, but the ethnic background of its members also gives them a certain status within the broader society. This status by and large excludes them from the complex power-sharing network characteristic of Uzbek society. On the other hand, direct association with the former colonial power (which has lingered on well beyond the collapse of the USSR) bestows upon them some privileges commonly associated with education, professional competence, and freedom from strict social conventions.

Foreigners visiting Uzbekistan find themselves farther up the scale; they are almost universally treated as guests of honor and respected for their apparent "expertise" or better living standards, but they are even less likely than the Russians to be included in the sophisticated communal life that forms the backbone of Uzbek society.

CUSTOMS & TRADITIONS

HOLIDAYS AND FESTIVALS

Holidays and traditional festivals are important in Uzbek culture. They provide an opportunity to socialize within different communities and to reinforce personal ties between those communities. Of all such events, the national holidays are the most public and formal.

Only two proper Islamic holidays are officially celebrated in Uzbekistan: Eid-al Fitr and Eid al-Adha, known locally by different names (see below). Other Islamic holidays are not officially recognized as such, but are celebrated in mosques and in some families. Easter is the only non-Muslim holiday widely celebrated by the Russians. Followers of Judaism, Buddhism, Baha'i, and other religions celebrate their holidays in private.

NATIONAL HOLIDAYS

May 9 Day of Memory and Remembrance. Victory Day.

September 1 Independence Day. The most important holiday, officially solemnized on different days around this date.

October 1 Day of Teachers and Mentors

December 8 Constitution Day. Celebrated to commemorate the adoption of the new Constitution of independent Uzbekistan in 1992.

RELIGIOUS HOLIDAYS
Nowruz

The traditional Central Asian New Year's Day, a pre-Islamic solar holiday, is now celebrated on March 21, the vernal equinox, in a time-honored way. It is a celebration of awakening nature and the arrival of spring, rooted in the beliefs and rituals of Zoroastrianism.

The main ceremony takes place on the night of March 21, and before that day people tidy their homes, wash carpets, decorate their rooms with flowers, and may buy new clothes to visit relatives and friends. All housekeeping must be completed before the rising of the morning star on the day of Nowruz. The main ceremonial dish, *sumalak,* is made from sprouting grains of wheat, with flour and oil. The whole *mahalla*, mostly women, gather around a cauldron, all taking a turn to stir the mixture. When it is ready, and is still warm, the *sumalak* is given out to neighbors, relatives, and friends. Children enjoy the holiday because they often get presents of money, as well as blessings, from their parents and older relatives.

Eid al-Fitr

This Islamic holiday celebrates the end of the holy month of Ramadan, and is known locally under such different names as Hayit Bayram, Uraza Bayram, Ruza Hayit, or Ramadan Hayit. The date for the start of any lunar Hijri month varies, based on the observation of the new moon by the local religious authorities, so the exact day of celebration varies from year to year. In Uzbekistan it is usually one day earlier than in most other Muslim countries.

Celebrations last for three days, and at this time people go to see their older relatives and neighbors and visit cemeteries to commemorate their deceased relatives and tidy their graves. As an obligatory act of charity, money is given to the poor before performing the prayer that formally ends the month of fasting.

Eid al-Adha

Sixty-eight days after Eid al-Fitr is Eid al-Adha, known locally as Kurban Bayram. It commemorates the willingness of Abraham to sacrifice his son as an act of submission to God's command. An animal, usually a sheep, is sacrificed. The meat is divided into three parts. The family retains one-third; another third is given to relatives, friends, and neighbors; and the remaining third is given to the poor and needy.

Easter

The Orthodox Church celebrates Easter according to the Orthodox calendar, and it occurs in April or May, usually a week after the Western Easter. On the Saturday evening, a couple of hours before midnight, congregations gather at larger Orthodox churches. Most of them are not regular churchgoers, and some Muslims come along just to join the celebration. Many people bring boiled and decorated eggs and special cakes to be blessed by the priests. Everyone walks around the church in a solemn procession to celebrate the Resurrection of Christ, then goes inside

it for the service. On Sunday morning people visit friends and relatives, exchanging eggs and cakes and kisses, with the phrase "Christ has risen!" To many Russians this event is the sum total of their religious experience over the year.

EX-SOVIET HOLIDAYS

The authorities of independent Uzbekistan made a determined effort to remove all references to the country's Soviet past from public life, and that included the cancelation of almost all Soviet holidays. The first to go were the Day of the Revolution (November 7) and International Labor Day (May 1). Although Victory Day continues to be celebrated on May 9, in 1999 it was renamed the Day of Memory and Remembrance to include all the soldiers of Uzbekistan fallen in different wars. Constitution Day and the day of the Defenders of the Motherland, celebrated in Soviet times on December 5 and

February 23, have been shifted to December 8 and January 14 respectively.

Curiously, March 8, International Women's Day, little known internationally, was one of the most important holidays in the Soviet Union, and has stayed. It is common to give women gifts on that day, especially at work. With the absence of a parallel festival for men, Defenders' Day was used as a pretext to treat men with presents, but today some still do it on February 23, while others have moved on to celebrate manhood on January 14.

Of all the ex-Soviet holidays, by far the most popular and widely celebrated is New Year's Day, January 1. It has evolved from the Russian New Year and Christmas celebrations, and has retained such traditional elements as the Christmas or New Year tree, with a five-pointed red star atop; Grandfather Frost, with his granddaughter and helper the Snow Maiden; a traditional televised address by the president to the people, followed by a celebration that includes performances by favorite pop singers and professional dance troupes; the clock striking twelve; traditional snacks; and so on. In Uzbekistan, these attributes have been slightly modified: the red star has been replaced by the eight-pointed star or a bird, both used in Uzbekistan's state emblem, and Grandfather Frost's red gown has turned dark blue. The New Year's celebration is a good example of the wonderfully hybrid quality of Uzbekistan's urban culture.

INTERNATIONAL FESTIVALS

Apart from the festivals that are linked to international holidays mentioned above, there are only two internationally recognized holidays that have entered the mainstream culture in Uzbekistan, albeit with some controversy. These are Halloween and Valentine's Day, both gaining popularity with young people in larger cities under the influence of the global mass culture. However, in the 2010s the authorities launched a series of public campaigns against the celebration of "alien" festivals as "unsuitable to the local culture and mentality." Valentine's Day was declared as amoral, compromising the Islamic ideals of chaste and pure love. Halloween was simply labeled "foreign" and "unpopular," and Halloween parties, traditionally held in restaurants and nightclubs, were banned. This conservative backlash, however, had only a limited effect, and many young people simply celebrate these holidays in more private spaces.

UZBEK CUSTOMS AND TRADITIONS

In Uzbekistan "tradition" is a buzzword that is
used to explain virtually everything from the way
people dress, eat, and meet friends, to the principles
underlying attitudes to work, regulations, and
authorities. It neatly dovetails with the concept of
"national" and other such familiar terms from the
old vocabulary as "mentality," "character," "ancestors,"
"our people," and so on. Customs and traditions are
visibly evolving and changing before people's eyes,
but the current wisdom is that somewhere there is
an authentic core of "true" Uzbek traditions that has
always been there, hidden for a long time under a
thick layer of political, cultural, and other historical
circumstances, that is only now coming to the fore.

Although this is what many people believe, the

living reality of life in
Uzbekistan shows how
mutable and vulnerable
the seemingly solid
institutions of family,
neighborhood,
occupation, religion,
culture, and country
are. Yet, despite
the perpetually
transforming lifestyle,
people cling to
the customs they
remember from their
childhood and to
the belief that they
secure links with the
ancestors, the country's
eventful past, and its

age-old culture. This attitude is common among Uzbeks, less so in the Russian communities, but in general people like their traditions and are happily involved in the different ethnic rituals that often make up the only way to connect them to their indigenous culture, gradually receding under pressure from all forms of modernity.

The most traditional Uzbek ceremonies are associated with the rituals of transition—birth, marriage, and death. All these, to some extent, involve members of the community, from relatives and neighbors to colleagues and local authorities, and many guests of honor. Most are rooted in pre-Islamic and Muslim practice but have also been affected and reshaped by a century of secularism and other external influences—once mostly from Russia but today also by European, Turkish, Arabic, and Chinese material culture. For example, Chinese fabrics, which have different patterns and colors, are now often used to make Uzbek traditional dress. Other borrowings include the pajamas Uzbek men buy in the UAE, or plastic bathroom slippers that are often worn outdoors.

Most guidebooks on Uzbekistan and travelers' blogs tend to emphasize the role traditional rituals and customs play in the life of ordinary people. This is due to the distinct "otherness" of these rituals to a foreign traveler combined with the local rules of hospitality that apply to foreign guests, which may well result in visitors attending one ceremonial feast after another and being overwhelmed with their perceived exoticism. In reality, however, rather than exotic rituals it is the values and attitudes of the Uzbek people that characterize local culture.

Birth

Beshik-tuy (the wooden cradle festival) is the ritual celebration of putting a newborn baby in a cradle for the first time. Today it is usually held on the seventh, ninth, or eleventh day after the birth of the baby. The ceremony has some regional variations, and also varies according to the family's income. The relatives, mostly from the mother's side, provide the cradle (*beshik*), tablecloth (*dastarkhan*), cakes, sweets, and toys, and bring gifts to the baby's parents and grandparents. Everything is packed into cars or buses along with the guests to the sounds of local wind instruments, and the cavalcade drives to the family house. Traditionally the baby's grandfather receives the cradle. He passes it on to his son, who then gives it to the baby's mother. In the past, in order to signify pure thoughts, white flour was daubed on people's faces. This practice still goes on in villages, and white flour is often used in one way or another during other traditional ceremonies.

While guests are invited to the lavish table to enjoy the food and the music, in the next room the

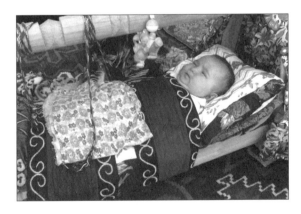

older women teach the young mother the way to swaddle and prepare the cradle for the baby. At the end of the ceremony the guests come to see the baby and give gifts, money, or sweets, which they place on the *dastarkhan* spread in front of the cradle.

In contrast, in Russian and other "Christian" communities, the birth of a baby is very much a private affair, and traditionally only close relatives are allowed to help with or even see the baby until it is forty days old. After that, relatives and friends may be invited to celebrate the event and the mother can now take the baby out of the house. These rules are becoming more relaxed with time.

For Koreans the most important celebration of a baby is not the birth. The twenty-first and hundredth days are special, but the main ceremony is when the baby is one year old. The day (*tol, asyandi*) starts with family rituals that involve traditional costumes and the custom of making the baby "choose its destiny" by picking up one object from several laid in front of it. The celebration may end in a restaurant with relatives, friends, and colleagues enjoying the event in a typical urban fashion with a lavish supper, loud music, dancing, and alcohol.

NAMES

Names in Uzbekistan can reveal a lot about a person's ethnic, social, and family background. Officially all names in the country follow the long-established Soviet pattern: family name, first name, and patronymic (a derivative from father's name), but since the end of the USSR this once unified system has become more diverse and interesting.

Uzbek names reflect the complexity of the country's rich and eventful history. Most names originate from Arabic (Akbar, Mukhtar, Fatima), Persian (Sherzod, Firuz, Gulsanam), or Turkic (Ugiloy, Pulat, Quvondyk), with the first having the highest and the last the lowest social status. In recent years it has become fashionable to change short Arabic names into more prestigious longer ones by adding such prefixes as Mir-, Sho-, Abdu-, or suffixes like -khon, -hoja, -jon, and to remove the Russian ending -ov from surnames, so Akbar Akhmedov might become Shoakbarkhon Mirakhmad. Uzbeks have also dropped the Russian ending for the patronymic (-ich and -ovna) and replaced it with -ogli for boys and -qizi for girls. Some Uzbek names reflect family history and circumstances. Twins are usually called Hasan and Husein (boys) and Fatima and Zukhra (girls). Girls may also have male names to reflect their parents' wish for boys (for example, Ugiloy, which means "son"). High child mortality generated such names as Tursun ("Let him stay") or Ulmas ("Does not die"). Children are never named after a living relative. Tajik names are similar to Uzbek names, with the exception of distinctly Turkic ones.

Russians have retained their traditional names (for example, Oleg Aleksandrovich Karpov), but recently the number of acceptable first names has shrunk to a handful that do not sound archaic or pretentious (such as Alexey, Pavel, Mikhail, Vladimir, and Sergey for men, and Olga, Ekaterina, Natalya, Elena, and Victoria for women). Most of these names have a Greek origin and parallels in other European languages, although some parents choose to emphasize their ethnic identity by giving their children distinctly Russian (Slavonic) names such as Yaroslav or Pelageya. Russian children are often named after their grandparents, or even parents.

Armenian surnames end with -yan or -yantz (Danielyan) and Georgian with -dze, -iani, -atia, -shvili (Maharadze, Kipiani). The Armenian Church is neither Catholic nor Orthodox, and most Armenians used to have traditional ethnic first names, such as Ashot, Asmik, or Grenik, but in the last century they started to borrow Russian and, for some reason, Shakespearian names, so combinations like Oleg Sarkisyan and Ophelia Nalbandyan are not uncommon. Georgians, who are Orthodox Christians, use their own names (Shalva, Vato) or versions of the traditional Greek names (Kote for Constantine, Sandro for Alexander).

Tartars may share some surnames with Uzbeks (Kurbanov, Abdurakhmanov) and Russians (Enikeev, Yusupov), and use their own versions of traditional Muslim names (Khanifa, Iskender, Nuriya) or adapted borrowings from European languages (Marat, Luiza, Renat, Venera). Koreans have a limited choice of surnames (most common are Kim, Li, Pak, Khan, and Chzhen) and usually have Russian first names such as the archaic Klimentiy and Afanasiy popular with older generations and Vadim, Stanislav, Yulia, and Natalya given to today's children.

In mixed families all the above traditions can be represented at once. Children may have a Russian name and an Uzbek surname, like Mikhail Rakhmanov, or "international" names acceptable for both families (Sabina, Diana, Ruslan) or, finally, official Muslim names (Botyr, Zikiye, Iskandar) and their informal Russian equivalents (Borya, Zina, Sasha). As each name has a meaning and a tradition behind it, people in Uzbekistan happily tell stories about their names.

CIRCUMCISION

Khantakilish, circumcision, commonly known as *Sunnat-tuy* (literally, the celebration of the law) is an ancient ceremony prescribed by Islam. This ceremony is traditionally performed on three-, five-, or seven-year-old boys, but in urban families there is a growing tendency to circumcise sons as babies (the practice followed in Jewish families). *Sunnat-tuy*, also curiously referred to as "wedding," is an elaborate ceremony involving many people and therefore requires preparations to be made ahead, including the accumulation of necessary means. A few months before the ceremony relatives and neighbors start sewing ceremonial quilts and preparing gifts. All this is entrusted to women who have many children.

Traditionally, the ceremony is held in the family home, but today many families celebrate it in large restaurants or public halls (*tuy-hona*). It starts with some prayers from the Quran recited by an imam, usually from the local mosque, in front of the elders of the neighborhood and relatives. The table is set, and the adults distribute token gifts to the children.

In the past it was customary to bring the boy to the ceremony dressed in bright clothes and riding a colt, a sign of his transition from boy to young man. Now, especially in cities, where most traditional ceremonies are held in public halls rather than family homes, this element is dying out. Still, everybody gives the boy money and sweets, and then the collected sum is spent on him by his parents or older relatives.

The circumcision is performed by a local medicine man (*tabib*) with traditional instruments. In the cities there is a trend toward laser circumcision. A lavish dinner with the ubiquitous *plov* (see page 117) ends the official part of the ceremony. Traditionally, in the evening, children and young people made a bonfire to play and dance around, but this custom, too, now seems to be on the wane.

ENGAGEMENTS AND WEDDINGS

Of all the traditional rituals, the wedding is by far the most important and ceremonial occasion in Uzbek culture. Paradoxically, it is also the one with most regional, class, and stylistic variations, ranging from three-day celebrations involving hundreds of relatives, neighbors, friends, and several homes to glitzy, one-day affairs with limousines, black ties, expensive bouquets, and staged photo sessions. Meant as a decisive projection of both families' social status and commitment to a certain lifestyle, weddings today combine the traditional element with modern aspirations, underpinned by the need to conduct both a proper religious ceremony (*nikoh*) and the official registration of the civil act of marriage in the Civic Registry, an institution inherited from Soviet times.

The official engagement (*fatiha-tuy*) is usually held at the bride's house, and involves

elderly people from the neighborhood, officials,
the mullah, and relatives from both sides; but not
the groom or his parents. The members of the
community and the matchmakers perform the ritual
of breaking the bread (*non sindirish*) and from this
moment the young people are formally engaged.
The ceremony ends with the appointment of the
wedding day. Each matchmaker receives a ritual
kerchief with bread and sweets and presents to pass
on from the girl to her fiancé and his parents. When
the matchmakers return to the boy's house, they
bring the gifts for examination by his relatives and
community. This ceremony completes the ritual
of betrothal. Between the day of *fatiha-tuy* and the
wedding day both families negotiate the dowry and
plan the ceremony. A few days before the wedding,
young people from each side hold traditional hen
and stag parties.

On the wedding day the bride's family holds a
party centered on the eating of the wedding *plov*,

which has been cooked in the house of the groom and then sent to the bride's family. A similar *plov* ceremony is held in the groom' home. These are important rituals, but are not the main part of the wedding ceremony.

The act of marriage consists of two stages. The imam of the nearby mosque reads the *hutbai nikoh* (prayer for marriage), after which the couple is declared husband and wife before God. After, or now often before, the *nikoh* the couple and their relatives go to the Civil Registry to register the marriage. In cities this part of the ceremony has a distinctly European flavor, as both bride and groom wear traditional Western wedding clothes, in which they visit memorials to the deceased (which may be a monument to the Second World War or to Timur) to lay flowers, and go to a park for a photo session.

The culmination of the celebration is the bride's ritual farewell to her father and other male relatives and her formal transition to the bridegroom's house. Once again, while traditionally the farewell took place in the bride's house, increasingly it takes place in a restaurant. The leave-taking ceremony in the restaurant can be attended by all the family, but only the bride's mother and her female relatives go to the groom's house. Today the party at the restaurant is seen by many as the most important public ceremony of the wedding. On the following morning, older distant female relatives from the bride's side examine the couple's bed sheets to find evidence of the bride's virginity. In most families this is taken very seriously, but in modern families its importance is dwindling.

The wedding ends with the ritual known as *kelinsalomi* (the bride's greeting) in which the bride respectfully greets numerous relatives and neighbors on the groom's side, who bring her gifts and wish her well. After this the wedding ceremony is considered over, and family life begins.

Russian Weddings

The traditional Russian wedding is not as elaborate or expensive as the Uzbek one, but it is different from the usual Western affair. There are no rehearsals, bridesmaids, or flower girls. Otherwise it's a noisy and entertaining celebration. The best man and the maid of honor are known as "witnesses," and the registration of marriage takes place at the Civic Registry, although some couples also choose a church ceremony, which requires catechization. Traditional brides wear a long white dress and a veil, and grooms wear a dark suit.

After the official part, the bride, groom, and some close friends and relatives tour the historic sites of the city, taking pictures and drinking champagne. This is just a prelude to the main event, which includes music, singing, dancing, long toasts, and an abundance of food and drink. It is now quite common to have the wedding reception in a restaurant, with a toastmaster (*tamada*) to announce performances, give the floor to those who want to propose a toast, and organize entertaining contests for the guests and newlyweds. This, and some other aspects of the Russian wedding, have been adopted by other urban cultures, to different degrees.

The Morning *Plov*

An interesting Uzbek ceremony known as "the morning *plov*" is traditionally held on one of the three wedding days or as a ritual of commemoration (a year and twenty days after a death) or, increasingly, as a social event. It takes place early in the morning, so that all the participants have time to get to work. The organizers of the ceremony agree on a date and time with the *mahalla* and send invitations to relatives, neighbors, and friends. On the evening of the previous day, the rite of *sabzitugrar* ("chopping carrots") is performed by neighbors and close relatives. The morning *plov* should be ready by the end of the morning prayer (*bomdodnamozi*). Guests sit at the table, read prayers, and drink tea, after which the *plov* is served on large plates. After the meal the plates are removed and the guests read prayers again; they then leave to make room for the next visitors. The morning *plov* ceremony usually lasts for one to two hours and is served by men only. As with many other Uzbek ceremonial meals, its main objective is to reinforce social ties and mutual commitments.

BIRTHDAYS

Traditionally, birthdays were not celebrated among Muslims, and some religious families still ignore them, but this custom, introduced by the Russians, seems now to be happily embedded in different ethnic communities. Birthdays are celebrated in families, with friends, and at work. Generally they are more important for young people, and give them an opportunity to show some independence by inviting whoever they want or by asking for particular gifts. A birthday involves a special cake and presents from parents, relatives, friends, and colleagues; being essentially a Russian tradition, it is less of a neighborhood event than an Uzbek celebration would be. Gifts can range from flowers, chocolates, and cosmetics to smartphones, laptops, and even a car. Important birthdays are sixteen and eighteen (when a child formally becomes an adult), "jubilee" ones such as twenty-five and fifty, and sixty-three for men, as this was the age when Prophet Muhammad died.

FUNERALS

Funerals are the most conservative occasions in Uzbekistan. Uzbeks and other Muslims follow the Muslim practice with some local features. The body is washed and wrapped in a white shroud inside the home. Women mourn in the courtyard and men, in traditional gowns and skullcaps, sit outside, meeting visitors. The mourning colors are dark blue for men and some combination of white and blue for women.

In the Uzbek tradition it is essential to bury the dead on the day of the death. Women do not go to the cemetery, no matter whether the deceased was male or female; only men see the dead off on their final journey. At least part of the funeral procession is made on foot, and strangers who happen to see it will often join in to help carry the stretcher on which the body lies, for at least seven steps. The grave pit has a crevice (*lahd*) where the body is placed. The burial is conducted by the mullah, who reads prayers (*janaza*).

For three days the family of the deceased receive visitors. Meals are not prepared in the house; neighbors and relatives take over this responsibility. Commemoration ceremonies are held on the seventh, twentieth, and fortieth days after the death, and another on the 365th day.

Unlike many other rituals, Russian funerals are more complex and require more time for preparation, following the Eastern Orthodox tradition. The body is buried in a coffin, but the traditional period of three days between the death and the funeral is often reduced to one day because of the hot climate. The traditional mourning color is black, and women often wear black headscarves. Visitors come to the house to say their farewells; many people follow the procession to the cemetery and return to the house, and there is a commemoration ceremony involving several traditional dishes and drinks. People propose toasts in memory of the deceased, but never clink glasses. Similar ceremonies are held on the ninth, fortieth, and 365th days after the death.

Armenians take funerals even more solemnly than Russians, and men do not shave for at least forty days after the death of a relative.

Cemeteries combine several cultural traditions and often feature elaborate and expensive tombstones that include an engraved photograph of the deceased.

SUPERSTITIONS
People in Uzbekistan combine atheism, religious faith, and superstitions in various measures and mixtures. Certain superstitions are shared between different groups; some are community-specific. Conspiracy theories, nontraditional forms of medicine, witchcraft, shamanism, fortune-telling, and simple superstitions "just in case" permeate everyday life in Uzbekistan in a way many visitors find slightly baffling, in that they may influence otherwise rational or even official procedures.

SOME UZBEK SUPERSTITIONS

- Bread should be kept "face up" at all times.

- Things should be bought in pairs, not in odd numbers.

- Never cut your fingernails outside your home; it is bad luck.

- Bundles of pepper pods or branches of spiky plants ward off evil spirits. So do old shoes, which are often nailed above the entrance gate.

- The evil eye can be averted by wearing a tiny Quran at the neck or special blue beads with a white "eye."

- Ill-wishing neighbors can cause you harm by placing sand or broken needles in front of your house.

- A mullah, or any old person, can help to avert the evil eye or bad luck, cure the sick, mend a relationship, and so on, by reading a prayer in Arabic.

- Do not eat or shake hands with others using your left hand.

- You must slaughter a rooster or a sheep before an important event, such as moving to a new home or office, or when someone is ill.

- Horsemeat sausage increases male potency.

SOME RUSSIAN SUPERSTITIONS

- A broken mirror or spilled salt brings bad luck.

- A birthday party should be held on or after one's birthday, not before.

- Before leaving the house on a long journey, you must sit for a moment in silence.

- Unmarried people should not sit at the corner of the table, or they will never marry.

- If someone sneezes while telling something, it means they are telling the truth.

- Never whistle inside a house.

- A stranger should not look at a newborn baby before it is forty days old.

- Accidentally breaking a glass is good luck. At weddings it is done on purpose after registration.

- If a fork or spoon falls on the ground, you can expect a female guest. If a knife falls, expect a male guest.

- If you are not recognized when seen or heard, you will be rich.

People often borrow superstitions from other communities and usually do not take them too seriously unless an important event is concerned, when all the rituals must be observed.

chapter four

MAKING FRIENDS

Friendship is important in Uzbekistan, but its nature and value depend on the community or subculture. Traditional Uzbek culture gives more weight to family and neighborhood links, so your closest friends are often your cousins or neighbors. In the same kind of family, it is only boys and men who are allowed to form true and free friendships; girls are closely controlled by their parents, and then by their husbands, and their only chance to make friends outside the close circle of relatives and neighbors is at school.

In a less traditional setting, friendships are more flexible and cordial. Particularly strong are different forms of male bonds, which often reinforce existing communal, university, or corporate relationships. Men-only parties are common, sometimes accompanied by liberal amounts of alcohol, but women still find it more difficult to develop friendships outside their family context, even in the cities. Friendships between men and women are much less common among Uzbeks than other nationalities, and are not encouraged. Friends made in youth are for life; later relationships tend to be more context specific. Some nationalities, like Koreans and Uzbeks, tend to choose friends from their own kin, but ethnically heterogeneous companies in cities are very common and offer opportunities for friendships across the ethnic and cultural divide. However, if you don't speak Uzbek or Russian, language will be a problem (see page 154).

ATTITUDES TOWARD FOREIGNERS

In Uzbekistan a foreigner is seen first and foremost as a guest of honor, with all the positive and negative implications that this status carries with it. You are looked after; you go to different formal and less formal parties, lunches, and dinners to eat great quantities of food and drink toasts to friendship, Uzbekistan, and everybody's health and success. You are treated with respect and care—maybe a bit too much. People are interested in your country and your family and ask all sorts of questions, which do not require elaborate answers. They are eager to ask you about your impressions of their country, and always pleased to hear how much you like it. Usually the higher your social position, the more honor and attention bestowed upon you. People in Uzbekistan are generous, hospitable, and friendly, but this attitude is not exactly friendship. It is based on the deeply ingrained sense of duty to welcome guests, to represent one's country and community in the best possible light, and to provide a warm atmosphere for social interaction and small talk.

In a business context a considerable amount of time is spent on this kind of social interaction—the human side is always present. Even people who occupy an official position will sooner or later reveal a human face if you encourage it. For example, if a police officer stops you to check your passport, you may well end up talking about a common friend— not unusual in a society where everyone knows each other—or a recent football match. Even in a legal dispute, a person may refer to family or other circumstances, whether or not it is strictly relevant to the case. In general, you always try to build a relationship and negotiate rather than stick to the rules.

At the same time, it is not easy for a foreigner to break into the inner circle. A consequence of being a guest of honor is that you remain an alien unless you establish some common interests and affections, which is not easy for a Westerner in a traditional Uzbek community. Often there are few common topics to discuss, apart from family and food. Many people, especially the older generation, have a limited understanding of or interest in Western life. The situation is better in multicultural urban communities and with younger Uzbeks, who are more ready to embrace global culture and more likely to share values and topics of conversation with Westerners.

MEETING THE UZBEKS

In the past, the place to socialize with Uzbeks used to be their home, which is still the case in many situations, although in the large cities more and more people now prefer going to cafés and restaurants. Most such establishments can be divided into two groups—Uzbek, and others (see pages 119–20). The former serve traditional Uzbek dishes at a low price, usually to a large number of people in simply but brightly decorated halls and

rooms. Today most public ceremonies that are not held at home take place in such restaurants, some of which function exclusively to host large parties (*tuy-hona*).

Other restaurants, cafés, and bars vary from local fast-food eateries and scruffy beer places to stylish bars and high-end themed restaurants offering various national cuisines, where many companies go for a good time. Some are open till late. It is always better to go to such places with a friend who knows the local scene, as they tend to change owners, styles, and clienteles quite often. In Tashkent and the tourist cities (Samarkand, Bukhara, and Khiva) there are restaurants and bars frequented by tourists and expats that are the least authentic but probably the most comfortable places for all sorts of cross-cultural encounters.

Nightclubs are rare, and locals may see them as "little havens of freedom," which also means that the things people do there can get quite intense.

The same can be said about different semi-underground bars frequented by local artists and hipsters, which offer an interesting if not always the most sophisticated cultural experience.

SOCIAL LIFE AT WORK

Relationships between colleagues in Uzbekistan depend on many factors, the most important being the type of organization they are working in and the social, ethnic, and gender makeup of the personnel (see pages 50–51, 60–61). Governmental and monoethnic organizations are more hierarchical than others, and the relationships between employees tend to be more formal, especially between officials of different rank. In certain professions, such as teaching or tailoring, which employ mostly women, there is a visible gender imbalance that affects the nature of social relations within the organization. More ethnically, socially, and gender-diverse organizations usually have flatter power structures and more flexible and open relations between colleagues. The same can be said about private businesses and international bodies, which reflect modern global work practices.

Uzbeks tend to merge formal and social relationships at work but often prefer to hide it in public. An outsider or a newcomer to an organization may initially receive a cold and formal reception only to discover human warmth later. These blurred borders between the person and the function contradict and complement the hierarchical nature of Uzbek society. They may result in excessively informal and boisterous corporate parties, or in the long lunch breaks that are sometimes taken at the workplace. Colleagues join in traditional Uzbek celebrations, birthday parties, national festivals, and other events. Such celebrations may be split, with colleagues first gathering together at work before joining their families at home. Generally speaking, Uzbeks working together like to have a good time, but a foreigner will probably feel more at home in a company that includes people with different backgrounds.

TOPICS OF CONVERSATION

The Uzbeks are masters of small talk. They try to avoid controversial, polemical, or opinionated discussions, especially in public or with strangers. Most common conversation topics are related to family life. People can chat for ages about relatives and friends, marriages, births of children, graduations, promotions, health issues, and so on. In recent years over two million labor migrants from Uzbekistan have moved to Russia and other countries, and this development has added another dimension to everyday conversation. Uzbeks enjoy finding common ground: common friends, relatives, places of study, interests, and so on. The first questions they ask strangers are probably about their marital status and children, which many Westerners may find socially awkward.

Another important group of topics revolves around money. Many people are concerned about their income and rising prices, dollar exchange rates, difficulties with using debit cards, and other such matters as what to buy, where to buy it, and at what price. Work is also often discussed, not as a process but in relation to its financial benefit. People ask each other about their salaries, although this has become less common in urban communities.

When Uzbeks talk about the weather, they often focus on the material consequences, such as late snow in spring that kills fruit-tree buds, or lack of rain for crops. People often compare weather in different years and comment on global climate change, but generally take a fatalist view of this. Most Uzbeks like spring and summer and prefer very hot weather to clouds, rain, or snow.

Politics has become more prominent as a topic of conversation, owing to the growing influence of the mass media and the Internet, but it is often more about Russia's foreign politics and the antagonism between Russia and the West. Influenced by Russian state propaganda, many Uzbeks take the Russian side even in its disputes with Muslim states. Local topics are discussed with some caution because of the opacity of local politics and a deeply ingrained reluctance to criticize the authorities.

Culture, art, religion, science, and other issues close to the top of the psychologist Abraham Maslow's "pyramid of needs" rarely figure in conversations with people who are not personally involved in such matters, aside from the highly educated urban classes. Even so, the people you'll meet casually in streets, shops, public places, taxis, and in small towns or villages usually come across as rational, commonsensical human beings. You can have a conversation with almost anyone about certain historical or political topics, and even if they are uninformed their opinions are usually

based on logical thought and a wish to have
a balanced viewpoint.

INVITATIONS HOME

The Uzbeks are hospitable, and it is not uncommon
to be invited to someone's home. If you receive an
invitation be sure to accept. A refusal is commonly
perceived as an offense, or an insult. Any visitor is
offered tea and snacks. Making and drinking tea plays
an important role in the Uzbek culture, and there are
certain rules that people assiduously follow.

Bring a gift, such as local sweets. If you know your
host drinks alcohol, a bottle of vodka or wine is a very
good present. For a formal event you are expected to
arrive on time, but for a less-formal occasion the rule
is relaxed. Remove your shoes and leave them at the
door. Be prepared to greet everyone with a handshake,
but with someone of the opposite sex wait for them to
extend their hand first.

The table will probably already have food on it,
as this is the traditional way of entertaining guests.
The meal may start right away, but before it begins
you may be offered soup, tea, or a shot of vodka
accompanied by a toast. If offered a drink, it is rude
to turn it down, and you may be asked to offer a toast,
which should include thanks to your host.

Once you get past the initial course, most of the
etiquette rules are over, or at least the expectations
are fairly relaxed for foreigners. The Uzbeks readily
forgive breaches of etiquette, but do your best to
watch what others do and follow suit. You may find
that the host will serve everyone personally, as certain
cuts of meat are reserved for certain people based on
their standing in the host's eyes. Unfortunately, this

means you have to eat what you're served, and, as a guest of honor in Khoresm, this could be a sheep's head. Usually, after each course your plate will be cleared away and you will be given a new one.

Depending on the context, use cutlery in the manner you prefer. On a formal occasion it is held in the continental style (knife in the right hand, fork in the left), but people are not fussy about whether you use only a fork or even only a spoon. Generally, fingers are used more than in the West; be sure to use only your right hand. Your piece of bread is placed directly on the table, and should be finished during the meal (using your right hand only). When the meal is over you may be served tea or another beverage, which you are expected to accept.

Tea

The Uzbeks usually drink straight green tea, but in Tashkent black tea is also popular. It's brewed in small round teapots, traditionally decorated with indigo and white floral motifs. The tea is poured into small handleless cups called *piala*, which you hold at the bottom and the rim. Uzbeks don't put sugar in tea but serve it with sweets, lump sugar, fruit, and nuts.

Before serving the tea, the host or hostess fills and empties a cup back into the teapot three times. The purpose of this is to mix up the brew and make it equally strong for everyone. Older people and guests of honor receive their cup from the host's hands, and you will notice that it is only half full. This is a sign of respect, and has several explanations. One is that it gives the hosts an opportunity to show their hospitality by treating the guests with more tea more often. By frequently asking for more tea, the guest demonstrates his or her respect to the family. Also,

it is difficult to hold the *piala* if it is full of hot tea, as you can easily burn your fingers, but a half-full cup is easy to handle and the tea cools down faster, while the remainder of the brew stays hot in the teapot.

The Russians have different ways of drinking tea. In the nineteenth century, tea in Russia was made by heating a large samovar, or kettle, over a coal burner, with a teapot full of a very strong brew atop. Such an arrangement meant that the hot water and tea were poured separately and mixed to taste in the cup. Although samovars have long disappeared, in many Russian families tea is still made in this way. Russians usually drink black tea from a glass, cup, or mug, often with sugar, sometimes with lemon, milk, or jam. Green tea is less popular but always available. Tea is served at the end of a main meal or separately, typically with sweets and cakes. Tea bags are rarely used in the home, but are widely used in cafés and restaurants. Younger people today drink less tea and more coffee, usually of the instant variety.

HUMOR
The Uzbeks are open and happy and enjoy having fun when they are relaxed in a familiar social setting; otherwise humor does not figure prominently in

everyday public life, when people prefer to come across as serious. Uzbek men may sometimes laugh in public, usually when they are with their peers; women only privately, when they are together. Uzbek humor is rich and situational, and involves little self-irony or wordplay. Russian humor is darker; telling jokes is one of the favorite ways of passing time in company. Uzbeks like jokes about different social settings, different ethnic groups, or people living in different regions of the country who are considered to have their own particular features to be laughed at. TV comedies are rough, physical, and include a lot of gaffes and one-liners. Though crude sexual jokes are rare, innuendoes about male–female relationships are not uncommon.

The Patriarch

A father of several children had always worried that his youngest child had red hair and looked quite different from him, unlike the other children. Every now and then he would ask his wife, "Look, I'd forgive you anything, but tell me one thing: is this ginger boy mine?" And the woman would answer, "I am telling you, he is yours, yours." But he was never convinced, and would ask the same question again. As his life was coming to an end, he called his wife to his bedside and said, "You can see I am dying, and you don't tell lies to a dying man. I will ask you for the last time: is this ginger boy mine?" "Don't worry, dear," said the woman, "I always told you the truth. He is yours, he is truly yours. The only one."

The New Husband

An Uzbek man married a Ukrainian woman and started telling her how she should behave in his presence. "Listen now, woman. Remember, when I come back from work, you must greet me and look at my skullcap. If it is tilted back, I am happy, and I will give you presents; but if it is tilted forward, beware—I am angry and will beat you." She replied, "Dear, listen. If you come back from work and see my hands on my chest, I will kiss you and give you food; but if you see my hands on my hips, remember, I don't care which way your skullcap is tilted!"

MANNERS

Most of the behavioral restrictions in Uzbekistan are based on the Islamic faith. To a degree, people also maintain the Soviet mentality, as they rarely involve themselves in other people's personal affairs, and tend to keep to themselves in public. Owing to this attitude, people rarely take offense. Although everyone will notice odd behavior and cultural abnormalities, seldom will anyone point out your cultural mistakes.

In addition to observing the dress restrictions mentioned below and following local table manners, the most important behavioral restrictions tend to be common sense. As mentioned above, avoid sensitive topics such as politics, money, religion, and business unless initiated by your local counterpart, and avoid being loud, rude, or drunk, or showing off about wealth.

Foreigners may find themselves uncomfortable with certain local manners, such as questions about your marital status, or being stared at, but remember that these are nearly always from genuine curiosity rather than a wish to intimidate you.

TABOOS

There are many taboos in the Uzbek culture, although they are not as rigorously imposed as in many other Muslim societies. Like everything else in Uzbekistan, they are dependent on context, and often what is right in one situation will be wrong in another. Most of these taboos have Islamic origins or are related to generic Uzbek customs and traditions.

As relations within and around the family are particularly important for the Uzbeks, a number of taboos regulate these relations and prevent deviations from the established norms. One set of taboos formalizes the social hierarchy and the attitudes of respect. It is considered very rude not to add *-opa* (for a woman) or *-aka* (for a man) to an older person's name, even if the person is only two years older than yourself. So, Matluba would be Matluba-*opa*, Karim would be Karim-*aka*. If you do not know the person's name, you can just say *opa* or *aka*. These terms have found their way into the local Russian culture, where it is also common to call strangers *brat* (brother) or *sestra* (sister).

Another group of taboos regulates gender relations, especially restricting girls' freedom of behavior and association in the name of public morals and righteousness. Girls should not dress too frivolously, talk too much, maintain eye contact with their elders, especially men, walk around unaccompanied, or make friends without their parents' consent. The same rules apply to married women, who are also not supposed to do "men's work," which involves hard physical labor, such as gardening, or to communicate with other men, such as when buying meat (see page 107). In traditional parties or events such as funeral ceremonies, men and women often sit in separate rooms.

Many taboos relate to food and meals. Like other Muslims, many Uzbeks do not eat pork or drink alcohol, and some will not sit at the table where these products are served. People wash their hands thoroughly before a meal. Local flat bread (*nan* in Uzbek, *lepyoshka* in Russian) is broken by hand and not cut with a knife. In a family, the father eats first, and the children will not think of touching food before him. The same applies to the guest of honor. It is also considered bad manners on the part of a host to fill a guest's teacup more than half full, as it means you want the person to leave. It is impolite to turn down food, which is difficult at a meal that may consist of several full courses, so people usually eat a little of each course.

Traditionally, Uzbeks did not have pets and kept livestock outside the home. In cities today this is no longer the case, and urban Uzbeks have happily embraced the global pet-keeping culture.

These traditional taboos are more relaxed outside the family context and in the cities, and may be applied selectively, depending on the situation. Particularly interesting are the cultural mixes at men's parties, where traditional Uzbek ceremony merges with the Russian masculine subculture, involving pressure to drink vodka and deliver long toasts, a duty one is not supposed to avoid. In a multicultural context, both Uzbeks and Russians are quite tolerant and flexible about their taboos, and normally do not insist on their strict observation.

There are taboos on certain topics of conversation. With their strong emphasis on social harmony, Uzbeks try to avoid the exchange of any negative information, and are masters of the kind of small talk that involves asking questions to which only positive answers are expected. Consequently, the topics of death, poor health, conflict, divorce, money problems, and so on are usually avoided in public. For the same reason people usually do not talk about politics, religion, or anything that may provoke a clash of opinions. With any forms of public disagreement discouraged, Uzbeks rarely take principled positions or express strong opinions on topics outside their traditional discourse.

On the other hand, people are willing to ask questions and discuss some issues that may be considered taboo in the English-speaking world. Everyone is interested in your marital status and how many children you have. You may be asked questions about your house, your family, and your salary, but if you prefer not to discuss such matters you can give elusive or superficial answers; such questions are usually asked to establish some kind of common ground, and if this purpose is achieved there is usually no need to go into details.

DATING

Dating can be tricky, as different rules apply in different contexts. In general, traditional Uzbek society is strictly against dating, especially without any prospect of marriage; but, as usual, the reality is somewhat more complicated. As in many cultures, sexual behavior is guided both by what is regarded as acceptable—arranged marriage, no intercourse before marriage, and so on—as well as by a set of informal rules that people rarely explicitly discuss.

Contemporary urban culture, however, somehow brings these two codes together, resulting in an interesting mix of expectations and underlying principles. Usually gender roles are asymmetrical and can be defined as "macho men, girly women," with certain deviations from this informally prescribed norm. Men are possessive and dominating. They are expected to pay all the costs of a date, such as taxis, meal, and drinks. The attitude toward their girlfriend in public is that of confidence, strength, and a mixture of old-fashioned courtesy and disregard: they often behave in a way they would not tolerate in their partner—drinking spirits, flirting with other girls, or spending too much time with their buddies.

Women typically try to use the best of "Western" and "Eastern" gender etiquettes, avoiding responsibilities as much as possible. They like a man to respect their individuality, which may come in the form of various whims rather than claims for the right to make their own decisions. One of the inalienable rights of a woman on a date is to arrive late. City women are usually well groomed, feminine, and elegant. They spend a lot of time, effort, and money on their looks, but would much prefer at least some of the investment to be covered by their partner. While maintaining their independence, they usually shun many of its less pleasant aspects, such as being financially self-sufficient, looking after their own safety, and carrying their own bags.

Of course, the rules are much more relaxed in today's multicultural urban communities. For a foreigner, it may be easier to pick up a woman in a city in Uzbekistan than even in Europe or the US, as sexuality is clearly used as one of the few ways in which people can express their individuality, and where they can enjoy a level of freedom that they may find it hard to achieve in the surrounding social reality. Dating here is therefore often about forgetting things and taking a break, about a little escape from reality, rather than about fun for its own sake, but it can offer a rich and exciting cross-cultural experience.

PRIVATE &
FAMILY LIFE

HOUSING
The Traditional Uzbek House

In rural areas, towns, and most suburbs, the
standard type of family house is still the traditional
Uzbek building, based on the concept of a courtyard
more or less isolated from the outside world by a
blind wall. Made of adobe, baked brick, or concrete,
the house usually accommodates an extended family
including several children and grandparents. Most
of the rooms are located on the ground floor except
for a section directly above the entrance gate called
bolohona (balcony). The rooms are split into men's
and women's areas, and usually lead from one to
another in a row. Most of the windows face the inner

courtyard, and are covered with blankets. Furniture is kept to a minimum, and thick, quilted duvets (*kurpacha*) are used as mattresses, cushions, and blankets, as Uzbeks spend a lot of time on the floor, sitting or lying around a low table. Colorful carpets cover the floors and are hung on the walls. Spacious yards usually have several fruit trees, a vegetable plot, a sheep or cow pen, a basic toilet arrangement, and a large trestle bed.

The Colonial Russian House

Although the years of Russian/Soviet rule are rarely referred to as "colonial," the period has produced a distinct style, and its architecture has left an indelible mark on the look of Uzbek cities. The earlier (late-nineteenth-century) houses were made of unbaked brick, and looked very much like provincial Russian houses, with a main entrance, a corridor and sitting room close to the entrance, and a couple of bedrooms and a kitchen at the back, with a terrace facing a small yard. With an array of old furniture and shabby artifacts from the Art Deco period, these houses offer an unexpected perspective of the cross-cultural lifestyle in Central Asia. Large houses built from the 1920s to the '50s in the style commonly referred to as "Stalin's Empire" usually display the same characteristic features as the colonial housing, but on a grander scale, with high ceilings, heavy wooden doors, storm windows, and thick brick walls.

Soviet Apartment Blocks

The ubiquitous, uninspiring, rectangular blocks of brick and concrete that dominate the residential areas of the larger Uzbek cities were intended to be only temporary dwellings when they were first constructed in the 1960s.

However, as the prospect of Communist victory was becoming more distant than ever, this approach to the construction of residential housing was developed further to result in a number of designs of four- to sixteen-floor concrete houses grouped in so-called "microregions."

Modern Housing

After a nearly twenty-year hiatus, the government resumed its house-building program, combining all the above styles in various proportions. The new high-rise buildings feature large, expensive apartments that cost almost as much as a detached house; the new houses for farmers are built and painted to an established standard; and multiple private houses in the previously colonial parts of Uzbek cities merge the features of the Uzbek traditional, Russian colonial, and international (also known as "European") styles in an interesting way that has yet to be clearly defined by historians of Central Asian architecture.

DAILY LIFE AND ROUTINE

Daily routines in Uzbekistan vary depending on which side of the rural/urban divide you are in, your occupation, social class, income, and cultural preferences. Traditional Uzbek families go to bed early and wake up early. Women must do the housework in the morning before it becomes too hot, and farmers have to start working or travel to cities to sell their produce at bazaars.

In the cities, life is governed by the need to get to work by 9:00 a.m. and back home by 6:00 p.m. five or six days a week. Government officials tend to stay late at work, and the middle of the day is quite relaxed, especially in the hot season.

While in the past most Uzbeks preferred to stay at home in the evenings, and would go out only on special occasions, in recent years an increasing number of people have developed a taste for eating out. Many, especially young people, are ready to try foreign food, although local cuisine remains most people's favorite. Most restaurants and other establishments close at 11:00 p.m., which gives the impression that there is no nightlife in Uzbekistan. In fact, there are a number of bars and clubs that carry on quietly with their business, trying to attract as little attention as possible. Here, as in many other cases in Uzbekistan, a local friend or contact is crucial to open the door. After that things get much more relaxed.

EVERYDAY SHOPPING

Uzbeks take shopping seriously and always try to get the best possible price. The most traditional and popular place to shop is an open-air market or

bazaar, with stalls selling vegetables, fruit, and other homegrown produce. Vendors of the same kind of produce are grouped together, and openly compete for customers, offering free samples and discounts. Seasoned customers walk from one stall to another and bargain over the prices. Russians and other minorities are less skilled at this, and foreigners usually end up paying more than locals no matter how hard they try, but local products are in any case very cheap by international standards. Traditionally, most shopping at bazaars is considered men's work (although they may be accompanied by their wives), as there is a lot to carry back home for a large family. Certain items, such as meat, are not supposed to be bought by women at all. They may buy light snacks and sweets on special occasions, but in general, Uzbek women are discouraged from doing the shopping, especially alone.

Most bazaars have small shops around the perimeter selling cheap clothes, shoes, household utensils, stationery, DVDs, and various prepacked or imported food products. Some shops seem to sell them all, and there are kiosks with tiny windows through which you never see more than the person's hands. Sometimes little "markets"—essentially tables or blankets on the ground—appear outside metro stations and in the street. Everything, from vegetables to faucets to single cigarettes to fresh meat patties, is sold out of large shopping bag.

At the other end of the spectrum are the increasingly popular supermarkets and shopping centers that have popped up in all the major cities. They sell mostly imported goods and prepacked local produce at twice the bazaar price, but are the preferred choice of the middle classes who don't mind paying a "third-world premium" price for a wedge of Camembert or a bottle of cold-pressed olive oil.

Women tend to spend more time doing this kind of shopping than men, but this distinction is much less evident in the younger generation. Urban teenage boys have happily embraced consumerist culture, and follow the fashions by shopping in a way that makes their parents shake their heads in disbelief.

MEALS

Uzbeks generally still prefer cooking and eating at home. A traditional home meal begins and ends with tea. If there are guests the host decides where they should sit, and only then he and his family take their seats around the table. The place of honor, reserved for family elders or guests, is at the end opposite the entrance to the dining room. Usually several generations of the same family living in one household eat together, and older people are treated with particular respect and care.

In conservative homes, mainly in the villages, men and women eat separately, but in the cities this practice is observed only on religious holidays and at funerals. Usually the whole family sits at a large table and the host or the oldest person at the table reads a short prayer, after which everyone may start eating.

An Uzbek breakfast is usually very simple, and consists of coarse bread, butter or sour cream, sugar, sweets, and tea. In recent years, Coca-Cola and cheaper local varieties have become very popular.

A typical Russian breakfast consists of tea or coffee, bread and butter with jam, cheese, or sliced sausage, boiled or fried eggs, and frankfurters. This may be cut to just tea with sweet cake or pancakes (*bliny*). Semolina, wheat, or buckwheat porridge (*kasha*) is no longer as popular as it was in Soviet times. Russian culinary influence on Uzbek families has become more evident recently as hundreds of thousands of migrants from Uzbekistan move each year to Russia, while others are coming back, although the influence is limited. Some middle-class urban families have reluctantly opened up to Western breakfast options, such as muesli, fresh fruit juice, water, and salad, but this is still very unusual.

Lunch tends to last long, and even at work many people manage to break for lunch early and come back late. This is when the Uzbek staple, *plov*, is commonly served. Uzbek men prefer their traditional, calorie-rich food for lunch, and often eat together in cheap canteens and street cafés. Uzbek women are more likely to try out new kinds of food, and some middle-class women are health conscious. Nevertheless, in the modern context lunch is often regarded as the main meal of the day, to be shared with relatives, friends, or colleagues, even if it clashes with the need to maintain working discipline. Consequently, lunches are long and on special days, such as Fridays, or when there is a family gathering, people may quietly skip the rest of the working day. Almost all social occasions and celebrations are, in effect, an extended form of lunch.

Supper, traditionally the main meal of the day, is usually eaten at home. Guests are invited only on special occasions. Typically, families eat together and the food is quite heavy by Western standards. It is usually based on the same traditional dishes, but these days may be less elaborate than lunch. It is still seen as more important as it reinforces family links.

CHILDREN

It is important to have children, preferably several, including at least one son. Childless families are generally seen as an anomaly, or as a sign that someone—generally thought to be the wife—is infertile. Children, even boys, are usually brought up by their mother with the help of other women in the family. The father's traditional role of breadwinner limits his contribution to particular responsibilities such as giving gifts and administering punishments.

Children are taught to obey their parents and to respect everyone older than themselves, and in this way they learn from a young age to obey their seniors and rule their juniors. While this system provides little opportunity for them to develop their own individuality, personal interests, and capacity  to make decisions, it makes them socially adaptive and involved in all the activities of adulthood that they will later repeat. Therefore, most young Uzbeks are worldly, communicative, and obedient; they often have similar interests, values, and behavior to their parents' and are capable of making decisions, taking responsibility, and acting in a familiar traditional setting. However, as individuals they may be somewhat immature, with little interest in self-fulfillment or the world outside their community.

In the cities, especially in multicultural communities, families are more exposed to different cultures and children have many more opportunities for personal development than in villages. Urban parents are usually well aware of the need to provide their children with education, social position, and means. It is therefore not uncommon for middle-class children to attend two or three additional courses, such as English, math, and tennis; to be interested in computers, cars, and foreign countries; and to wish to travel and gain higher education.

EDUCATION

Children attend school for nine years, from the ages of six or seven to fifteen, and can go on to professional colleges or lyceums. Colleges are institutions of vocational education in such areas as IT, construction, banking, transportation, and so on. Lyceums prepare students for further academic studies, and are often affiliated with universities and other institutions of higher education. There are gymnasiums, boarding schools, and special schools for students with disabilities. The school attendance rate and the quality of education in rural areas are lower than in the cities, although the government has been trying to address this issue. Primary and secondary education are free, and the government subsidizes some expenses for students from poorer families. The language of instruction in schools and universities is Uzbek or Russian, although teaching in Karakalpak, Tajik, and other minority languages is available in some schools.

To enter a university or institute, candidates take the University Entrance Test on the same day across the country, usually August 1. Sometimes there are additional examinations, for example, in conservatoires. Top candidates study free of charge; some receive a modest scholarship; others must pay fees. Students study for four years toward a bachelor's degree and, if they wish and can, two more years for a master's degree.

The government is making efforts to bring the educational system into line with international standards by reforming teacher training, and student-centered classrooms are gradually being introduced into Uzbekistan's schools and universities. However, many teachers still follow the Soviet teacher-centered model, with a lot of old-style lectures and dictation and not much group work or class discussion.

Because higher education is generally regarded as a means to social advancement, this affects student life. Parents often choose colleges and universities for their children and make them spend a lot of time studying. This pressure and external motivation applies to both schoolchildren and university students. Apart from a couple of international educational establishments, there is little social life in Uzbek universities, which is limited mostly to sports clubs and celebrations of official holidays. Students usually socialize by going to clubs or having parties in their homes.

THE PATH TO MARRIAGE

There is strong pressure to marry young—usually between the ages of eighteen and twenty-two, or around the time of finishing college or university. Uzbek marriage is a predominantly communal event, carried out in coordinated and negotiated stages involving relatives from both sides performing prescribed roles. As the time approaches, a young man's parents ask for recommendations of a suitable young woman for him to marry, aiming at a match that would be beneficial to both families. When a candidate is identified, an older woman from the man's mother's family, or another woman of the same status, visits the young woman's family to meet her parents and hold preliminary discussions. If they agree to take it further, she may obtain a photograph of the potential bride to show the family when she reports back. All being well, the first meeting between the young people is usually arranged now. At this stage any arrangements can be canceled with no harm done; but this cannot go on for ever, for with each such setback the pressure grows on all sides to be more "accommodating"; the midwife's reputation is also at stake. If the young people like each other this is regarded as a sign for the procedure to enter the next stage, and matchmakers are sent to arrange the engagement (see pages 75–6).

MILITARY SERVICE

There is conscription for young men aged eighteen, which lasts a year. There are some exemptions and alternatives: the only son in a family is exempt, and service can also be reduced, for a fee, to a month's intensive training. There are, however, more candidates than the army needs. Many young men from rural areas enter full military service for the privileges that it brings, such as eligibility to serve in the police force or other law-enforcement agencies.

TIME OUT

LEISURE

Uzbeks enjoy relaxing in company, and family events and holidays offer plenty of opportunities for this. In recent years having a get-together and a meal in a restaurant has become popular, and in the main cities there are bars, discos, nightclubs, and bowling alleys, but they are not numerous, and tend to close by 11:00 p.m. Restaurants and bars range from expensive to cozy to cheap to scruffy, and a recommendation from a local friend will help you to choose, or sometimes even to get access to some of them.

Water parks and swimming pools are popular in summer. There are fitness centers, a handful of paintball clubs, and even a golf course near Tashkent, but the most popular sports facilities are the small, open-air soccer pitches to be found in residential areas.

In Soviet days young people were organized in special-interest clubs in so-called youth centers, and some of these continue to operate, catering to a wider public. There are music, dancing, cookery, and singing clubs. Young people, as everywhere in the world, are into computer games, but board games such as chess and backgammon are still popular, especially with older Uzbeks, who enjoy playing them in traditional teahouses.

Although the opportunities for leisure may seem limited, many are simply not advertised and the key, as in most other aspects of social life here, is a good local friend who will take you around and introduce you to others who share your interests.

EATING OUT

According to Islamic law, the consumption of pork is forbidden. Pork is, however, available in some restaurants. If you are dining out with traditionally minded Uzbeks, play safe and don't order pork or pork products. Some Uzbek Muslims do eat it; most don't.

What surprises many visitors is that alcohol, introduced by the Soviets, is part of daily life. Only strict Muslims and health-conscious young urbanites refrain from drinking alcohol. While traditional Uzbek cafés observe the prohibition on pork and rarely sell alcohol, in more expensive restaurants there is a wide choice of food and drink. Smoking is common, and men smoke a lot more than women do.

UZBEK CUISINE

One entrenched stereotype about food in Uzbekistan is that it is either oily, high-calorie, meaty Uzbek food or bland Soviet-type fare. While this may be true in cheap everyday cafés, Uzbekistan can offer a real culinary experience. You only need to know where to find it. Although Uzbek food predominates, it is usually cooked at home, and cafés and restaurants tend to offer only a narrow range of popular dishes. The country's

cultural diversity, especially in the cities, however, means that the local culinary palette consists not only of Uzbek and Russian food, but also many Korean, Tartar, Ukrainian, Jewish, Armenian, Georgian, and Uighur dishes. On top of that, in Tashkent and the larger tourist cities there is a growing number of restaurants serving international food—mostly Turkish, Italian, Japanese, Chinese, and Eastern European.

Traditional Uzbek cuisine was based on local produce and did not include the now common potatoes, tomatoes, cucumbers, lemons, eggplants, cauliflowers, many kinds of greens, or sunflower oil until after Russian colonization. There is a great deal of grain farming in Uzbekistan, so bread is a staple, as well as rice. Mutton is popular. There

is a wide variety of dairy products, mild spices, and interesting vegetables, including turnips, horseradish, chickpeas, and yellow carrots. Meals are eaten with baked bread (*nan*), of which there are different varieties.

Uzbekistan's favorite dish is *plov* (*palov*, or *osh*), a main dish made with rice, mutton, thinly sliced carrots, and onions. It is usually cooked in a cast-iron cauldron over an open fire. Garlic, chickpeas, eggs, raisins, cumin, barberries, or quince may be added for variation. Although often prepared at home for family and guests by the head of household or the housewife, the best *plov* is believed to be made in enormous cauldrons, sometimes serving up to a thousand people on special occasions.

Other popular dishes include *laghman* (boiled mutton with noodles, vegetables, and broth), *shurpa* (mutton soup), *chuchvara* (dumplings), *jiz-biz* (fried mutton slices with chips), *damlama* (sautéed vegetables), and the ubiquitous *shashlyk*, or kebab, which comes in many varieties from the regular mutton pieces to the more esoteric sheep's testicles and pieces of liver. The only salad that has entered the Uzbek home kitchen is *achik-chuchuk* (or simply, *achuchuk*)—tomatoes and thinly sliced onions.

These make up the staple diet of traditional Uzbek households, but most urban families borrow dishes from other traditions. Popular soups include the Ukrainian *borsch*, based on beets, other vegetables, and meat; the Russian cabbage soup *shchi*; and the spicy Georgian *harcho*, with mutton, rice, and tomatoes. These and most Uzbek soups are chunky, and contain separate pieces of meat and vegetables.

The wide variety of salads found in middle- to top-market restaurants include not only the international favorites Caesar and Greek salads, but also many Russian specialties. Olivier salad, a traditional dish for the home New Year celebration for Russian people, has boiled diced vegetables seasoned in mayonnaise with finely ground sausage, while *vinaigrette* includes diced cooked vegetables (beets, carrots, and potatoes) with some sauerkraut and chopped onion.

DRINKS

Tea is available at cafés and restaurants, with or after the meal (see pages 93–4). Coffee is mostly found in expensive modern cafés and restaurants. There are local varieties of cola, which are popular.

The consumption of spirits, as in all post-Soviet countries, is more widespread than in the West, but is not as ubiquitous as in Russia. Most men drink vodka or brandy, commonly referred to as cognac. Some younger city types prefer whiskey. Women occasionally drink, but much less than men, and often opt for wine. Semisweet or sweet wines are often preferred to dry. The local wines, although drinkable, are not usually up to international standards. Some people still make their own wine, *samogon* (a kind of grappa), and various fruity liqueurs at home. Many people drink beer, thanks to its lower alcohol content and thirst-quenching properties—important and highly enjoyable in hot weather. There are some good breweries in Tashkent, Samarkand, and other cities that produce varieties of

lager, ale, and stout, with unfiltered beer among everyone's favorites.

Attitudes toward drunkenness in public vary, depending on the type of establishment, clientele, and overall context. It is usually tolerated in beer bars, nightclubs, and small local bars, where people come to relax in an informal setting, but is frowned on in traditional cafés and stylish restaurants.

RESTAURANTS

There are several different types of restaurant. The cheapest and most popular ones, called *oshxona*, serve only a limited variety of staple Uzbek food such as *plov*, *laghman*, or *shurpa*, commonly known as "national dishes" (*milliy taomlar*), a couple of salads, *shashlyk*, bread, and green tea. Their interiors are simple and often shabby, but the service is usually prompt and they offer value for money—if you like the food, that is.

Soviet-style cafeterias, often referred to as *bistros*, are commonly found near large offices, factories, and universities. These display a range of ready-cooked dishes that you pick up and place on your tray while moving in a line along the food bar. The choice of food is based on Russian cuisine with some local additions, but its quality, as to be expected in canteens serving precooked food, is fairly basic. However, they offer a variety of affordable foods in a short time.

In the main cities there is a growing number of more expensive restaurants, which vary from overpriced garish establishments to excellent places with interesting food and a great ambiance. Usually you will not need to reserve a table or wait to be seated. Most aspire to international standards, but only some have menus in English; others may have photos of the dishes printed on the menu. In the past it was common to be given a long menu of many different items, only to discover that most of the dishes listed were not available. This practice is gradually disappearing. Most restaurants add a "service charge" to the bill, but the phrase is misleading as it is just another way to increase the price and doesn't reach the pockets of the waiters. So, be sure to tip the waiter.

TIPPING

Tipping is common in restaurants, cafés, at the hairdresser's, and wherever a personal service is provided. Workers in communal services are not well paid, and tips help them make ends meet. The best way is to add something to the amount due without attracting attention to it, such as leaving the waiter about 5 to 10 percent.

TABLE MANNERS

The traditional Uzbek way of eating, sitting on the floor with food arranged either on the special cloth called a *dastarkhan* or on a low table, is still common in many families, in rural areas in particular. Some traditional restaurants offer this option by placing a small, low table on top of a large wooden bed called a *tahta*. Everybody sits or reclines around the table, although Westerners may find this uncomfortable.

In traditional dining style, there is usually a lot of food set out, and the hosts regularly encourage the guests to eat more. *Nan* is broken into pieces that are either piled together or laid on the cloth near your plate or bowl. Everything is eaten with bread, which comes in handy for soaking up the remains of your soup or for moving pieces of food on your plate. Although a lot of food is eaten by hand, the spoon is the most common piece of cutlery on an Uzbek table. Not only soups but all other kinds of food, including salads, are eaten with a spoon. While soup bowls are individual, some dishes, such as *plov* or *shashlyk*, are generally served on a large platter (*lagan*) for people to share. Salads and other foods are served in a large dish or bowl but are eaten off individual plates.

In a multicultural setting, sharing food is still common, especially salads, chips, and bread, but everyone has their own plate and the main course is ordered individually. Everything, apart from soup, is eaten with a fork. Bread comes in a basket. The use of a knife and fork is reserved for formal occasions, although it has become more usual with the young urban generation. Cloth napkins are rarely provided, but a stack of paper napkins is common.

PAYING FOR THE MEAL

Who pays for what, and on what occasion, is a big issue in Uzbekistan. Traditional celebrations such as weddings and birthday parties are usually covered by the hosts, but in recent years a kind of combined payment by hosts and guests has become commonplace. In general, although people in Uzbekistan may find it hard to make ends meet, they don't want to be perceived as needy. When two or more friends dine together, they may want to pay individually, which requires an additional calculation of service charge and tips, or they may split the bill equally. If someone "invites" you for a meal it means they intend to foot the bill. The best strategy is to accept your host's hospitality with only modest protestations, and allow him to pay—but to reciprocate later with a similar offer or a gift.

On a date the man should pay for everything. If a woman insists on paying her share she is making it clear that she doesn't regard the meal as a date. If a man is not generous—a cultural error that Westerners often make—either this is seen as a kind of disgrace, or the occasion is simply recognized as not being a "date."

ART, MUSIC, AND THEATER

Art

Broadly speaking, there are three types of art in Uzbekistan—decorative and applied, classical modernist, and contemporary. Old examples of the decorative and applied arts, including ceramics, jewelry, illustrated manuscripts, woodcarvings, and textiles, can be seen in museums. You will find many modern examples of these in the bazaars—a revival of traditional crafts has created new interest and a new market. From blue-and-white ceramic dishes and bright golden-thread embroidery to intricately carved gourd snuffboxes, engraved copper lamps, and hand-forged daggers, Uzbek artifacts attract both local and international customers.

Classical art in the form of oil paintings, watercolors, drawings, sculpture, and design is another by-product of the colonial past. By the mid-twentieth century Uzbek art was an amalgam of impressionism, modernism, and some distinctly Central Asian features. Classically trained Uzbek painters and sculptors have contributed to the current look of Uzbek cities and public building interiors.

Contemporary art, with its provocative message, has never had many followers or much support in Uzbekistan, but a handful of artists have gained international recognition. Their works encourage a critical view of the Soviet past and the post-Soviet present, the grand narratives inherited from the twentieth century, and modern cultural practices.

Museums and Galleries

There are several art galleries and interesting museums, but the most important one is surprisingly located not in Tashkent but up north, in Nukus, capital of Karakalpakstan. This is the Savitsky Museum, home to the second-largest collection of Russian and Uzbek avant-garde paintings of the twentieth century.

In Tashkent there is the spectacular Temurid Museum, celebrating the cultural legacy of the fourteenth to the sixteenth centuries; the State Museum of Arts; and other museums, including the open-air Railway Museum. Each of the main historic cities of Uzbekistan has its own museum of history and arts containing important exhibits, such as Samarkand's Afrosiab Museum and the Regional Studies Museum in Bukhara, on the site of its ancient fortresses.

The two largest galleries are in Tashkent: the new National Art Gallery of Uzbekistan and the Academy of Art of Uzbekistan, which stages regular exhibitions of Uzbek artists and the Tashkent Art Biennale.

Music

Music is omnipresent in Uzbek society. It is there, from the lullabies sung to an infant in its cradle to the ancient laments heard at funerals and commemorative

ceremonies, from the pop music blasting at you from passing cars to the rock bands playing in hipster bars. Some traditional Uzbek tunes (*maqom*) are thousands of years old. Many of the instruments producing these stirring notes have remained largely unchanged throughout the centuries and resemble older forms of the lute (*oud*), cello (*gijak*), and guitar (*rubab*).

Western classical music was brought to Uzbekistan by the Russians. The local classical music scene has developed into an interesting blend of classical orchestration and local musical tradition.

Yet it is another kind of cultural mix—modern local pop music, sung in Uzbek to Westernized folk tunes—that follows you everywhere. Catchy, easy to dance to, and completely innocuous, it is supported by the authorities as a safe alternative to other contemporary genres—from rock to electronic music—with their angst and disturbing subtext.

Theater
There are several Uzbek-language and Russian-language theaters, of which the State Academic Great Theater, known as the Navoi Theater, is the largest, and is best known for its ballet and opera. Others include the Khamza Academic Theater, which produces plays in Uzbek, and the Russian Drama Theater for Russian-speakers. The Ilkhom Theater is the hub of local avant-garde and contemporary art, and the Youth Theater is another ambitious establishment that seeks to merge musicals and spectacular performances based on traditional characters. All these are in Tashkent, and although provincial capitals also have theaters, they don't have the same status and attract fewer people.

SPORTS

The most popular sports are soccer, tennis, martial arts, and wrestling, including the local folk wrestling style, Kurash. There have been several Uzbek world champions in wrestling, boxing, and weightlifting.

Apart from professional sports, there are dedicated amateur sports clubs in most large cities, and a skiing and snowboarding community in Tashkent, thanks to its proximity to the Chimgan Mountains where there is a ski resort. Other popular sports include mountain climbing, hiking, biking, and paragliding.

BAZAARS

In a world where business transactions can be almost devoid of human contact, Uzbekistan's bazaars are a reminder of how vibrant and exciting trade can be. The bazaars are no mere collection of shops. They are the dynamic center of the community, a place where not only goods, but also news, culture, and politics are exchanged. Here, people trade out of doors, placing their goods on stalls or on the ground. You can find almost everything from fresh fruit and vegetables to hand-tempered knives, handmade musical instruments, ceramic bowls, and painted cradles. The vendors will tell you all about the products they sell. If something you fancy costs more than you were planning to spend, you can always strike a bargain.

Popular purchases include porcelain teapots, ceramic dishes, wooden bookstands, miniatures, silk scarves and shawls, thick quilted coats, clothing made of *ikat* and *adras,* rugs and carpets, old Soviet badges, medals, and busts of Pushkin and Lenin. Books printed before 1965 (and objects made before this time) are considered antiquities, and cannot be legally taken out of the country.

BARGAINING

Bargaining is expected in the market and in many private shops. It usually goes on for a while—it is common to show emotion, leave, come back, and/or ask around until the price goes down. This can be fun if you have the right attitude, so don't think of it as only a means to save money. In most tourist shops, vendors usually quote a figure of about twice what they might settle for, but as a foreigner you are unlikely to be able to bring the price down to this level. However, use the strategies just described plus your own sense of humor. Private shops may also try to charge a little more, especially on handmade products. A good local friend can help, but remember that local tour guides usually get around 10 percent commission from vendors, so they may be interested in helping you buy things at a low price but they have their own interest as well. In the bazaars the same rule applies, though you may be less likely to haggle away a significant sum.

CHANGING MONEY

There are two exchange rates for hard currency: the official and the black-market rate. The official rate is used in the economy, but as a visitor you may find it only in banks. The local currency is the soum (also spelled "sum" or "som"), and the banks will happily sell you soums for about double their real market price. However, selling and buying hard currency in the market is technically illegal, and there have been reports of foreigners being set up doing this. The difference in exchange rates can be substantial, although from time to time the government tries to bring them into alignment. Seek advice from a good local friend who knows the right people. Taxi drivers bringing you from the airport may offer to change money, but they never give you a good deal, so if you have to do it change only a little. Although most dealers accept roubles, euros, pounds, and other currencies, your best bet will be US dollars. The bills should be clean, whole, and have no stamps or writing on them.

WHAT TO SEE
Architectural Monuments
Uzbekistan is famous for its architectural monuments, ranging from ancient fortresses in the desert to majestic mosques and *madrasas* concentrated mostly in the tourist centers of Samarkand, Bukhara, and Khiva (see pages 20–23). Interesting colonial buildings can be seen in Bukhara, Samarkand, Tashkent, and in cities in the Ferghana Valley. Early- and late-Soviet architecture includes the early Constructivist main building of Samarkand University and the Modernist-Imperial Navoi Theater in Tashkent designed by Alexey Schusev. Although tourist brochures and travel guides focus mainly on Islamic architecture, Uzbekistan's cities are a mixture of distinct architectural traditions interwoven in a complex multicultural knot.

Places of Natural Beauty
Uzbekistan's cities are situated in oases formed by the deltas of its major rivers, but the spaces between the cities offer more exciting landscapes. There are the mountains of Chatkal and Chimgan near Tashkent, the Zeravshan range separating Samarkand from Shakrisabz, the Nuratau Mountains, and the huge Baysoon region with its unique folk culture. The vast Kyzyl Kum Desert ends with the Usturt Plateau, with its otherworldly plain and steep karst escarpment. There are thirteen nature reserves in the country, as well as other protected areas, each with its own characteristic flora, fauna, and geographical features.

chapter seven

TRAVEL, HEALTH, & SAFETY

Uzbekistan inherited many infrastructural merits and drawbacks from the Soviet Union, and, since Independence, elements of what were once known as the First and Third Worlds have crept into various fields, contributing to its rather patchy systems.

In general, the experience of traveling across the country varies enormously. The options range from up-to-date and highly efficient rail and air services to overcrowded old minivans and even donkeys— although the last are not always available these days.

While means of transportation and your physical comfort may vary, what will probably remain constant is the willingness of people to talk to you, to help you, or at least to respond to your queries. This will be less obvious in airplanes or fast trains than in minivans or country buses, but you will find that people in Uzbekistan like to strike up conversations with fellow passengers.

INTERCITY TRAVEL

Tashkent is the transportation hub of Uzbekistan, in particular for air travel, with flights that connect it with the country's provincial capitals and major cities. However, Uzbekistan has a fragmented and uneven distribution of population (see page 12), and in some places the transportation system can be somewhat irregular.

By Air

Currently, daily flights connect Tashkent with Uzbekistan's major cities that typically take thirty minutes to an hour. However, direct flights between these cities are rare, and to get from, say, Termez to Urgench, one has either to fly via Tashkent or to choose other options, such as traveling by car.

Uzbekistan Airways, the country's state-owned air carrier, operates a decent fleet of Boeings and Airbuses from clean, well-guarded airports. While security checks in the airports may be reassuring against possible terrorist threats (which are very low in Uzbekistan), they are annoying and can considerably slow down all the stages of clearance. This is much more likely in the case of international arrivals than in local terminals.

One of the peculiarities of flying in Uzbekistan is that local citizens can pay in soums, while foreigners pay in dollars. This is not so much discrimination against the latter but a kind of privilege for the

former; on paper they pay the same amount in hard currency, but for the locals this is calculated using the official exchange rate, which is usually much lower than the "real" one (see page 128). Electronic booking and check-in can also be a problem, but the situation is improving. There are many ticket offices in cities where you can book and buy tickets, usually for cash. There are no low-cost fares or last-minute discounts on tickets.

By Train
Until recently, the railway system in Uzbekistan was uncomfortably split into several disjointed sections, as parts of the regional network passed through the territory of the neighboring former Soviet republics, now separate national states. The situation was remedied by the mid-2010s, and now you can travel to almost any part of the country by train without leaving its own territory—although some links are far from straightforward. While Tashkent has a modest local railway network, other places each have just one train station, away from the city center.

There are several Spanish-built fast trains connecting Tashkent with such cities as Samarkand and Karshi, and more are planned. Some railways are powered by electricity, but most remain suitable only for diesel engines. Apart from the cheaper relatively modern trains made in China, there are plenty of old Soviet coaches that usually run at night, and are equipped with coal-heated water tanks to make tea, served in glasses in a metal holder. There are several daily trains connecting Tashkent with the main cities of Uzbekistan, but, unlike air tickets, you can buy railway tickets only at the train station or in one or two ticket offices in the city center. You need a passport to buy the ticket as well as to get on a train; actually you will need both the ticket and your passport to pass the security check on entering any major railway station. An electronic online booking system was introduced, but at the time of writing you still need to pick up your printed booking confirmation from the station. You pay in soums, in cash or with a credit card.

Night trains have separate compartments with sliding doors and four beds; the day trains offer different interiors with leather seats or wooden benches depending on the destination and class. The fast trains resemble airplanes both in the seating arrangement and in the type of service available on board, but as it takes only two hours to get from Tashkent to Samarkand, they offer the least opportunity to socialize with other passengers. The night trains, on the contrary, seem to be full of people wishing to share with you the story of their life, their sandwiches, or their bottle of vodka. So there is a different kind of fun to be had in Uzbek trains—but fun it is.

By Car

By far the most popular way of traveling between different cities in Uzbekistan is by car. People like cars, and see them as a necessity as much as a status symbol, but also as a flexible alternative to the rigid, timetable-driven public transport system. Each city and town has an area where drivers gather with their cars to offer themselves for hire. They pay no taxes and have no license, and yet they are tolerated by the authorities, who still have to come up with a competitive legal alternative to this informal, chaotic, but useful service.

In a way, such an arrangement is closer to a bazaar than to the kind of formal taxi service favored by Westerners and Russians, and it nicely suits some traits of the Uzbek national character. There are no timetables and no lines, but a lot of bargaining about cars, fares, seats, destinations, and all possible variables. A car departs as soon as it has three or four passengers. Sometimes drivers take a parcel or letter to deliver to the city of destination, in which case they can leave before the car is filled up. They may cheat you by saying, "I already have two passengers waiting to go," to lure you into their empty car parked at the back of the parking lot, but you can trust them with possessions and money. On the road they will tell jokes, listen to loud Uzbek pop or Russian rap, speak on their cell phones, stop to buy some local produce from vendors or refuel the car, share popcorn or sweets with you, and in short do everything possible to make your experience of being driven from one Uzbek city to another lively and unforgettable.

Roads and Traffic

Other than motorways, thoroughfares, or main city streets, roads in Uzbekistan can be described in terms from average to awful. Only major roads are maintained, and others, especially those deep inside communal areas, are left to the elements. There are cracks, areas of missing asphalt, pits, dust, gravel, and patches, and even in exclusive areas where there are large private houses the roads may be quite bad. Drivers complain but stoically lumber on. Everybody expects the authorities to fix the problem.

In cities, especially in Tashkent, main roads are regularly overhauled in the course of area redevelopment and are well maintained. In recent years, there have been multiple road-building projects, involving widening existing roads, creating new ones, and building new bridges and underpasses. These measures have been hastily undertaken to deal with the traffic jams that began threatening Uzbek cities in the 2010s.

The number of car owners has been steadily growing in recent years, mostly thanks to local car giant GM Uzbekistan, which churns out more than 200,000 cars every year. It became clear that the cities, built in colonial and Soviet times, were ill prepared to cope with this upsurge. The response focused mostly on the development of the road network, including the removal of trolleybuses and streetcars from city streets. Other measures attempted to impose stricter discipline on the road, but both approaches have produced only mixed results.

By all international standards, driving in Uzbekistan is not the worst in the world. It is a far cry from Cairo or Delhi, there is no *hagwalah*, or prank driving, as in Saudi Arabia, and no sixty mile traffic jams, as in China. Yet, considering the fact that Uzbekistan was part of the over-administered Soviet system, it is easy to see why many people feel that standards have declined, and the government is concerned about it. Road cameras, stricter fines, anticorruption regulations, and so on, have been introduced, but you still see drivers talking on their cell phones and passengers not wearing seat belts.

LOCAL TRANSPORTATION

It is fairly easy to get around most Uzbek cities, but it may not remain so for long. The cheapest, slowest, and least pleasant way is by bus, which has been the backbone of public transportation in Uzbekistan since the removal of environmentally friendly but clumsy trolleybuses and streetcars. Often overcrowded, buses remain the only option for many people commuting to the city center from suburbs in the morning.

The only city in Uzbekistan to have an underground train network, known as the metro, and until 2011 the only one in Central Asia, is Tashkent. The rapid transit system has at the time of writing twenty-nine stations on three lines covering mostly the central part of the city. As more and more people settled in residential areas on the periphery of the city,

the use of the metro has somewhat declined. Now the residents of these districts need a journey by bus to reach the closest station, but there are plans to expand the network. Each of the stations has its own artistic design and décor, and each travel guide of Tashkent lists its metro as a must-see. It is unfortunate that taking photographs inside the metro system or any of the stations is banned because they are considered military installations.

An interesting transitional form of transport from a bus to a taxi, especially popular in smaller towns is the *marshrutka*, or "route taxi." It is a minivan for six to twelve people that travels along a fixed route at a fixed price, just like a bus, but that can be hailed by anyone on the road or asked to stop anywhere by a passenger inside, like a taxi. The type of minivan and the fare vary from city to city. These *marshrutkas* also take passengers on journeys between different cities. They offer a more flexible alternative to buses at a comparable price, but may be lacking in comfort.

Taxis in Uzbekistan come in different colors and shapes and at different prices. The most expensive and reliable is a call taxi, which belongs to one of the officially endorsed taxi companies. These are painted beige in Tashkent and yellow in all other provinces of the country. Some companies equip their cars with a GPS navigator and tracking system; others use more old-fashioned radio connection. In the provinces not all yellow cabs can be called by phone—their color indicates that they are simply licensed taxis. Then there is nearly everyone else. You stand by the side of a road and hold your hand up and soon someone will stop to ask you where you need to go and at what price. Only some of these will be occasional drivers going (or not going) in the same direction. Most of these people make a living in this way, and some pay a leasing fee for a car they have got but not yet purchased. In general, these taxis are safe but the drivers' knowledge of the city may be hazy.

WHERE TO STAY

Tourism is one of those industries in Uzbekistan that can be thought of as genuinely thriving, and the hospitality business is well developed, although the common restrictions and peculiarities that affect all business in Uzbekistan apply here as well.

Foreign visitors must register with the authorities within three days of their arrival. This restricts their choice of accommodation to a range of hotels and B&Bs who can do the registration. Obviously, there are more opportunities in the capital and tourist centers such as Samarkand or Bukhara. The large hotels in these cities were built in the 1990s-early 2000s for international hotel chains but were later nationalized. These still offer good value, but for a casual traveler the better

option will be one of the smaller, usually family-owned local hotels and B&Bs commonly designed with some "Eastern" flavor. As the quality of service may change with time, it makes sense to consult TripAdvisor or a similar service for up-to-date information. This does not mean that you cannot stay anywhere else; only that you need to renew your registration every seventy-two hours.

HEALTH

One of the advantages of hot and dry weather over a tropical climate is a lower risk of infection. Products that would rot and decay in Karachi will simply dry in Karshi. The lasting Soviet legacy also means that a range of infectious diseases that had once been widespread in the region were contained by the Soviet doctors and are no longer a threat. All citizens are inoculated against various infectious diseases in childhood.

In general, health risks and their treatment in Uzbekistan are comparable to those in other post-Soviet countries. Foreigners don't need any vaccinations in order to enter the country, and there are very few health issues to worry about. AIDS levels are low. The most common major health risks in Uzbekistan are sunstroke, dehydration, colds, and food poisoning.

There is a special clinic for foreigners in Tashkent, and many hospitals and clinics in other cities have modern equipment and capable doctors offering treatment and operations at a fraction of the price in the West. The free state hospitals are rather poorly equipped, especially in villages, where not everyone can afford the price of modern medicaments in the required quantity.

Some international clinics in Tashkent recommend travelers to take out medical insurance in their home countries, but in reality only long-term visitors do so, as most hospitals and clinics are not familiar with insurance requirements from abroad and will expect payment in soums up front. They are unlikely to be able to provide documentation in English.

Ambulances can be called by phone on 103.

SAFETY

Uzbekistan is a safe country, populated by hospitable people. There are no militants brandishing Kalashnikovs, or Islamists, or local militias, or warring clans, and you won't meet any thugs, armed mobsters, ethnic bandits, drug dealers, hoodies, chavs, or angry football fans in the streets of Uzbek cities. The police presence in all cities is very visible, especially in Tashkent.

Occasional problems may occur when a visitor loses the status of a guest and is seen just as a vulnerable alien, which is often a result of cultural misunderstanding. Examples may include a misjudgment of the degree of familiarity, such as while drinking with strangers in a bar or night club; misjudgment of intent, as in girls being sexually harassed for behavior they deemed innocuous but the perpetrators saw as inviting; or misjudgment of context, as in walking alone at night in a poor residential area with a high unemployment rate.

Another important area where misunderstanding may occur is that of drugs. Central Asia has a long history of recreational use of such drugs as cannabis and poppy, and although the former is sometimes used socially in the bohemian subculture and the latter as a medicine for old men in villages, drug use in Uzbekistan is strictly illegal and visitors are strongly advised not to attempt to buy drugs. The same can be said about the areas bordering on criminal, such as prostitution, the smuggling of antiquities from Uzbekistan or goods into the country, hard currency deals, and so on. Even if you meet locals involved in such activities with apparent impunity, as a foreigner you are much more vulnerable, and the best strategy is to avoid such contacts. Ultimately, the main reason for such unfortunate and potentially violent cross-cultural encounters is the lack of cultural awareness on both sides, and that is what this book seeks to address.

BUSINESS BRIEFING

chapter eight

THE BUSINESS ENVIRONMENT

The Uzbekistan economy has a centrally planned organization that closely resembles its late Soviet-era model. The dominant motive behind this choice is the need for social stability, which has dictated a very cautious approach to reform. The country's economy depends on the export of a few main commodities, such as cotton, vegetables, textile, gold, gas, and cars; this does not encourage any deep reform initiatives, and the volatility of these markets often makes the authorities go back to the familiar command economy system. From time to time the government

launches campaigns for monetary liberalization and privatization, with limited success. At the same time currency control restrictions limit the influx of foreign direct investment, which until recently was mostly confined to large, state-sponsored joint ventures with such giants as GM, BAT, and MAN. In recent years, the number of successful joint ventures has grown, especially in such areas as textile and agriculture.

On the other hand, Uzbekistan, one of Central Asia's largest nations, has significant agricultural, mineral, and energy assets, and is ideal for cotton production. Uzbek gold production ranks seventh in the world. Significant amounts of copper, uranium, and numerous industrial minerals are also in production. On top of this, Uzbekistan is in the world's top ten producers of natural gas. These resources provide the potential for future growth, and five thousand joint ventures operating in the country in 2016 prove that successful investment in it is indeed possible.

REGULATIONS

Uzbekistan is an overregulated country, especially in areas that many foreigners usually take for granted, such as freedom of speech or a political position. Internationally, the country has a low ranking when it comes to respect for human rights. There are lots of official and informal bans that create a complex system where different sets of rules apply in different contexts. Certain spheres of life look more regulated than they really are—for example issues related to residence, housing, taxation, and communal services—but these can be enforced; others, which seem to be relatively straightforward and free are, in fact, riddled with unexpected and hidden obstacles. Many business-related issues fall into the latter category.

Usually the laws regulating one or another aspect of economy, such as foreign investment, banking, entrepreneurship, and small- and medium-sized businesses, are relatively liberal, but they almost always contain a clause that nominates an administrative body responsible for the implementation of the law and further regulation. This gives the body (for example, Central Bank, or the Ministry of Finance) the authority to implement rules, requirements, and regulations that may seriously complicate business procedures. One of the consequences of this is that many matters have to be resolved on a one-off basis depending on many variables, including who is dealing with whom, what connections they have, and who the potential beneficiaries are going to be. Commonly it necessitates a reliable and well-connected local partner or associate who will be responsible for ensuring that the bureaucratic process runs smoothly.

LABOR MIGRATION

An important factor that affects the country's economy and demography in many ways is the presence of over a million (some say even more) Uzbek labor migrants in countries such as Russia, Kazakhstan, Turkey, or Korea. Most of these are manual laborers, drivers, communal service workers, or shop assistants who usually send a considerable amount of their earnings back home. In 2013 these remittances made up 12 percent of the country's GDP, which made the life of millions back in Uzbekistan economically easier. On the other hand, with so many young men away, the demography of Uzbekistan was affected so that many women were left

without the means to support themselves or without
a prospective husband, which made them look for
different kinds of independent employment—a situation
unthinkable ten or fifteen years before.

As the number of labor migrants began to decline
following economic crisis in Russia, their income
also went down from US $6.670 billion in 2013 to
US $3.059 billion in 2015, and many young people
came back to Uzbekistan with limited prospects of
employment. Some of them brought back a new
awareness of the outside world; others returned as
more devout Muslims freed from the traditional
communal restrictions on radical Islam. All these
developments have given additional headaches to the
government, which has responded by trying to create
new workplaces for the returnees and by tightening
control over these potentially difficult groups.

BUSINESS CULTURE

Organizations range from the traditional, top-down,
bureaucratic hierarchies redolent of the Soviet era
to more modern local versions of international
multicultural businesses or NGOs. The defining
features of the business culture in these organizations
are the attitudes to power and the position of the
particular organization within the wide cultural
continuum—from Uzbek to Soviet to global culture.
Interestingly, power relationships and the underlying
culture may be quite independent categories. In other
words, you may encounter paradoxical combinations
such as extremely top-down power relations in a
local office of an international NGO, or cordial and
democratic business culture in a small, traditional
Uzbek business.

Office Life

As we have seen, different kinds of work ethic create slightly different working environments, but there are some common and seemingly contradictory tendencies that are present in any Uzbek office in one way or another. The power status of a person expands beyond their working duties, and rules that apply to a boss are more relaxed than the ones that their subordinates are expected to follow. However, age and working experience are valued and respected even if the person does not occupy a particularly high rank in the office. Working principles can be bent if it benefits social cohesion, but teamwork may suffer due to personal ambitions, and the ability to cooperate toward a common objective often depends on emotional, rather than rational factors.

Personal relations within the office are generally good, as people prefer not to air concerns in public and feel obliged to demonstrate regard and affection for each other. Yet this also opens up a wide range of opportunities for maneuverings and hidden agendas. Decisions are often made either by the boss or by consensus, as a purely rational consideration of alternative solutions may be seen as unhelpful, although emotional arguments are not infrequent. In more traditional organizations gender inequality can be more noticeable, but women are always treated with deference. There is a general agreement about what is right and what is wrong, and people can be quite judgmental; but there is also flexibility, mutual respect, and tolerance.

Business Dress

Men usually wear a formal suit or a tie and jacket, especially when dealing with government officials.

Casual business style may be suitable in less formal settings. Women in the office are particularly attentive to their looks and tend to dress up, with stylish clothes and makeup and high-heeled shoes. In government offices they wear a conservative business suit, a dress, or a blouse with a medium to long skirt. Trousers are acceptable but not neutral, as many Uzbeks still see them as a sign of female emancipation. Jeans, T-shirts, shorts, and other informal clothing are considered inappropriate in business, although in the hot months the rule is somewhat relaxed. In general, Uzbek office workers tend to dress more formally than Westerners. Crumpled jackets and a scruffy or "vintage" look are generally frowned upon. One should be well groomed, and clothing should be up to date.

CORRUPTION

Uzbekistan sits firmly at the bottom of all international transparency and corruption indices with other Central Asian countries and the likes of Nigeria and Cameroon. However, as we have seen, this is partly a legacy of the Soviet bureaucracy and partly a form of social cohesion, so important for all Central Asian societies. This means that the popular image of corrupt officials at the top exploiting everyone else is more than slightly misleading. People at all levels of society are involved in various kinds of informal social exchange that can be articulated or implied and which by no means always involves money. As a teacher, you are less strict toward your colleague's child in your class, as a traffic police officer you are more forgiving of your neighbor's careless driving, as a doctor you can ensure that your distant relative gets the best nurse in the hospital.

Another peculiarity of "corruption" in Uzbekistan is that it is often about hurrying along things that you are legally entitled to, not something criminal or otherwise morally questionable. In this way, it is similar to tipping for service that stretches beyond the restaurant and the barber. You tip a clerk for giving you a notification, or a communal service worker for doing a job well.

This does not mean that all corruption in the country is "soft." On the contrary, the type of social exchange described above provides a fertile soil for the abuse of power, fraud, bribery, and all kinds of sleazy deals at different levels. The government is trying hard to combat corruption by tightening control over all spheres of economic and administrative life through a complex network of committees, services, and agencies, but the overregulated public system in a country laden with so many contradictory regulations and little transparency continues to resist these efforts.

MEETINGS

As a foreign businessperson, you usually have to arrange to meet someone you need through someone you already know. It is possible to contact this person's secretary directly, but it is more efficient to have a local, well-connected intermediary. Alternatively, you may go through a special agency such as a Chamber of Commerce, but it is better arranged in advance.

First meetings usually take place in a formal setting. Top managers, like CEOs or ministers, try to be there on time, which is not always so with midlevel government officials, who are frequently required to participate in urgent gatherings called by their bosses.

It is common to shake hands before the host invites everyone to sit. Cards are exchanged at the beginning or at the end of the meeting. A typical seating plan is two tables arranged in a T shape, with the senior official at the top and the rest sitting in order of importance around the longer table. However, when meeting a foreign visitor, officials often prefer to observe the rules of hospitality and sit with them face-to-face at the center of a long table.

The senior official usually chooses and sets the tone of conversation, which becomes less formal by the end of the meeting, and even friendly at subsequent gatherings. Uzbeks are good hosts and want to you to feel welcome and relaxed, but this cordiality does not necessarily mean the negotiations will be an immediate success.

PRESENTATIONS

If you have to make a presentation, you should know your audience. Senior managers usually have no time for elaborate PowerPoint affairs; and prerecorded audiovisual presentations, although impressive, fail to establish the direct human contact so important in Uzbek culture. That said, such presentations might go down well with younger specialists in the subject. In most cases large groups of people will listen to a long talk out of politeness, without interrupting, but their attention span is relatively short. It is part of the culture inherited from Soviet times that senior officials read or give long speeches, but these are not intended to generate discussion or even questions. A formal monologue will fall into the same category and will generate little or no reaction unless someone in the audience has a particular opinion. Uzbeks perceive such lectures as top-down transmission of knowledge, and engage in discussion only if the gear is switched to a dialogue mode. Consider also the time needed for interpreting your speech into Uzbek or Russian.

In Uzbekistan, the value of working in groups or pairs in discussion as a means of generating

knowledge is not widely recognized, and it would be difficult to launch this kind of discussion without giving clear rules and explicitly defined roles to the participants. Normally, the only kind of interaction between presenter and audience takes place when the presenter deliberately lowers the degree of formality and indicates that they are seeking to provoke an argument. Jokes and familiarity with the local context can help to establish a genuine rapport, as well as self-irony, which is important if the presenter wants to dismantle the pedestal of a revered "source of foreign expertise" and start a conversation. In other words, the presenter has to convince the audience that expressing disagreement and asking questions on their side would not breach the rules of hospitality or be seen as disrespectful. This may take some effort. At the same time, it is important to avoid making oneself look silly and to remember that familiarity breeds contempt, or at least a lack of respect.

NEGOTIATIONS

This can be an interesting as well as a frustrating experience for a Western businessperson. In Uzbekistan, the culture of negotiations owes as much to the traditional practices of social encounters, including bargaining, as to Soviet-style administrative meetings. As a result, negotiations can be elusive, motivating, spontaneous, top heavy, tense, and contentious all at the same time. At times, you may feel as if you are being forced to accept a premeditated conclusion, the only subject of negotiation being the price. On the other hand, you may wonder at the sheer diversity of ideas and suggestions put forward, which may be tangential to the original agenda. Negotiations are also likely to be affected by urgency and delays, and certain decisions are made on the spot while others take time. In any case talks will be long and will require patience and understanding. When planning your strategy, there are three important things to remember: first, usually you are the source of capital and expertise while your local partners provide opportunities for their application; second, the social and emotional dimension of business relations is as important as purely economic considerations; and, finally, most decisions, even minor ones, are ultimately made at the top.

CONTRACTS

Uzbekistan's legal system is broadly based on Roman law, and is compatible with Continental business practice. Written and signed contracts are binding, and businesspeople take them seriously. However, the execution of the contract may be complicated by regulations issued by the body responsible for the supervision of such contracts. Contracts are usually drawn up in Uzbek, Russian, and English, depending on the context; large organizations and companies have lawyers familiar with commonplace international legal norms and can provide translation services at an acceptable level. There have been instances of legal disputes between international companies and government bodies regarding the execution of contracts that had to be resolved in the courts.

MANAGING DISAGREEMENT

Uzbek contracts always have a clause stipulating the way disputes should be resolved in courts, usually local ones. International companies often insist that an international arbitration court should resolve such disputes, as they suspect the local courts of being far from impartial. Some relatively recent high-profile cases of arbitration involved companies such as Newmont and Oxus Mining, but these cases are rare.

Disagreements in the workplace are better resolved informally and face to face rather than in writing or through a formal procedure. In the case of a cross-cultural disagreement, remember that Uzbeks are "we" people, sensitive to what they perceive as a criticism of their whole ethnic group or community. It is also important to avoid public confrontation in order to save face for all the parties concerned.

In any conflict you want to come across as a "real man" (even if you are a woman): emotional, or even angry, principled but magnanimous, never small-minded or impenetrably formal with no heart or soul. Take as an example Rudyard Kipling's *The Ballad of East and West*.

WOMEN IN BUSINESS

As a reflection of Uzbek patriarchal society, there are very few women at the top level of any organization, but they are often represented at middle management levels, and there are women who occupy positions such as lawyers and accountants. As a rule, there are good social and personal reasons for any woman to be in a position of power, especially in public administration: she might have started as someone's daughter, sister, or wife, but would  not have remained in the system without business acumen, resilience, and competence.

In private business the situation is somewhat different, as quite a number of women began their careers as shop assistants, shuttle traders, or schoolteachers, and developed into full-fledged managers. High levels of male labor migration have left many women with the need to support themselves and their families independently, while others simply feel that they can be more than just a housewife.

Both categories of women are treated with due respect, and, although their gender identity is acknowledged by colleagues, the traditional patriarchal attitude toward women normally does not affect professional relations.

chapter nine

COMMUNICATING

As we have seen, the rules of communication in Uzbekistan depend on the context. Uzbeks generally prefer to steer conversations along established and safe lines, avoiding negative or sensitive topics, while Russians tend to be more opinionated in a discussion, or even confrontational, when it concerns sensitive subjects such as politics. There is also a clear gender divide concerning topics and in the ways they are communicated, especially in the older generation. (See pages 89–90.) In young urban circles both ethnic and gender differences in communication styles are less noticeable, but they are still more distinct than in the West.

LANGUAGE

Although over a hundred languages are spoken in Uzbekistan and English is taught at school, language is still a problem when it comes to communicating with foreigners. For about 70 percent of the population, Uzbek is the mother tongue, and a further 10 to 15 percent speak it to a certain degree. Russian is spoken at a native-speaker's level by 15 to 20 percent of the population, mostly in the country's multicultural urban community and 40 to 50 percent of Uzbek citizens speak it as a second language. Assuming you do not speak Uzbek, speaking Russian will greatly increase your chances of being understood, as the percentage of speakers of English as a foreign language is little more than 5 percent—although this number is growing and the level of English is improving, thanks to the national program for English language development adopted in Uzbekistan in 2012. In the cities, especially in advertisements, these three languages may be mixed up on the same billboard without any particular logic.

Uzbek is a Turkic language with a great number of words borrowed from Arabic, Persian, and Russian, and it is the only official language in Uzbekistan. Its grammar and literary norms were consolidated only in the 1920s, and the differences between the spoken varieties and the official written language are considerable. There are also regional dialects with significantly different vocabulary and pronunciations that sometimes complicate communication between people from different regions.

From the 1930s to the 1990s the Uzbek language used the Cyrillic alphabet, and in the 1990s the Latin alphabet was introduced to replace the Cyrillic version by 2005, which has not happened. The Latin alphabet is still used only in titles, road signs, and textbooks, which confuses children who have to cope with two Latin (Uzbek and English) and two Cyrillic (Uzbek and Russian) alphabets, each with their different spellings for even mutually intelligible words.

Russian, an East Slavic language, is still spoken or understood to a different extent in all post-Soviet countries and is in effect the lingua franca in Uzbekistan. It lost its official status as "the language of interethnic communication" in 1991 and in the

1990s significant efforts were made to eradicate its use altogether, but it has proved more resilient than was originally thought. Ostensibly ignored by the authorities, it has gradually acquired a status similar to that of English in India and other former British colonies. No longer the property of Russians, it is still useful, especially in an urban and professional context.

GREETINGS

In Uzbekistan, greeting others can be quite an elaborate affair involving different types of physical contact and certain verbal formulas depending on culture, social context, gender, and age. Traditionally, Uzbek men shake hands with a slight bow, keeping their left hand pressed to their chest. Close friends and relatives usually hug, do a forearm grip, or even kiss each other. Women may shake hands with women but almost never with men. Russians and younger men simply shake hands with other men and may do a forearm grip. When two groups of friends meet, all the men shake hands with all the other men, but again, almost never with women, although it is quite common among Russians to greet women they know well with a kiss on the cheek. In an everyday office situation it is all right to greet others with a nod and the words of greeting alone.

The traditional Uzbek greeting is *Assalamu aleikum*, followed by a series of questions about the other's health, life, work, and so on that require no answer, but a reciprocal series of similar questions—a bit like "How do you do?" in English. In a less formal context the greeting is shortened to *Salam* and the question *Yahshi mi siz?* ("Are you well?").

The formal Russian greeting is *Dobroye utro/ Dobry den/ Dobry vecher* ("Good morning/day/ evening") or *Zdravstvuyte* ("Be healthy"), which is pronounced *zdrastuyte, zdraste,* or simply *zdrass,* the first being the most formal and the last the least formal version of the greeting. *Privet* may be seen as an equivalent of "Hi" in English.

STYLES AND STEREOTYPES

In the eyes of Russians and Westerners, the Uzbek communication style tends to be circuitous. Conversations may seem to be like a wandering path, with various hints and underlying meanings that are difficult to pick up on, especially through an interpreter—who, at the same time, may be helpful in explaining these undertones. This, as well as the desire to avoid negative subjects, may create the impression, especially for the Westerners, that Uzbeks "never say what they think." On the other hand, Uzbek people are emotionally open and positive; they appreciate sincerity and fun and easily switch to less ceremonial communication once the formalities are over. In this context, both Uzbeks and Russians commonly perceive the characteristic North European detached politeness as cold, "standoffish," and insincere. This impression can be reinforced by a visitor's desire to avoid topics that are considered too sensitive in the West, such as religion, ethnicity, personal relationships, and politics, and which are openly discussed in Uzbekistan—the only significant taboo being criticism of the authorities. This openness has a negative side too, as many opinions that are commonly expressed in Uzbekistan can be seen as patriarchal, sexist, racist, and prejudiced by Westerners, who often overestimate the universality of their own cultural norms.

BODY LANGUAGE

Most Uzbeks tend to be close talkers, and less than three feet (one meter) of personal space is seen as normal. People of the same gender can be quite tactile when talking. A woman might frequently touch another woman's arm, or sit very close to her. Men often have their arms around another man's shoulder, especially at parties, and hugging is common. Older people tend to be more tactile than the younger generation. Both men and women sometimes hold hands with friends of the same gender in public.

It's a different story with the opposite sex, although less so in multicultural company. There is typically more physical space between genders. At a traditional Uzbek party women and men sit separately, but even mixed and multicultural parties may at a certain stage break into gender groups so that women have a chance to talk about clothes and relationships while men discuss football and politics. Direct eye contact is common when interacting with peers of the same gender, but much less when talking to the opposite sex or to an older person or a boss.

Most Uzbek people like to look around them, and in the street will stare at anything they find interesting or unusual. Traffic accidents always attract onlookers, who will come to the scene and just stand there to watch what is happening. At the same time, in less traditional settings, such as in the underground train, most Uzbeks behave in exactly the same way as passengers in New York or London do—they stare into space, read, or get busy with their cell phones.

Personal space in the office is less clearly divided into private and public than in the West, and much of the space is shared. Unlike the norm in many Eastern countries, where sheer density of population limits personal space to a minimum, in Uzbekistan the defining factor is not lack of space but the communal lifestyle. Typically, such office commodities as tea, coffee, and sugar belong to everyone, and people chip in to buy them. Everyday mugs in a communal office kitchen may be personal, but there is always a large tea set for corporate celebrations.

GESTURES

Active gesticulation is more common among young men; women and older men tend to be more reserved. Not as expressive physically as Italians or Latin Americans, Uzbeks use gestures a lot. Here are some of the most common ones:

- As if you are washing your face with both hands—borrowed from a Muslim prayer—in everyday life marks the end or the beginning of something, such as a meal, a journey, or an exam, and so on.
- Pressing the right hand to one's chest is a sign of respect or apology, but also a greeting or farewell.
- The same gesture made with the left hand, while the right is used to point at something, to shake your hand, or to offer a cup of tea, is also a sign of particular respect.
- The index finger and thumb rubbed against each other means money or price.
- The index finger tapping the right temple means "a fool," or "stupid."
- Flicking a finger at one's own neck is either an invitation to have a drink or an indication that someone else is drunk.

TV AND RADIO

By the mid-2010s, all the previously active private TV channels and companies were replaced by state-owned TV corporations, which oversee the production of original content as well as the broadcasting and dubbing of foreign—mostly Russian, Turkish, and Korean—programs.

There are three major national channels, namely Uzbekistan (Uz TV 1), Yoshlar (Uz TV 2), and Sport (Uz TV 4). Two further channels, namely NTT and TV Markaz, cover only the central part of the country. A couple of channels focus entirely on Tashkent. Digital TV companies and cable TV services mostly re-translate a few major Russian and foreign channels, and each province in the country has its own local TV company. Many families have satellite TV with a wider choice of predominantly Russian and few international channels. Most national TV programs are in Uzbek, but some channels offer news or digest programs in Russian. The content of the material is by and large entertainment, with the emphasis on innocuous local pop music, talk shows, and popular TV series translated into Uzbek. The news programs tend to avoid in-depth analysis or even mentioning anything remotely controversial; as a result most of the urban population get their news from heavily biased Russian channels. In recent years, the number of previously available Russian channels has gone down, and starting in 2010, the cable TV services have had to use the signal only from a state-controlled company, Uzbekistan Cable TV, which broadcasts channels that contain no harmful or critical information about Uzbekistan.

There are several radio companies broadcasting in the FM format in Uzbek, Russian, and several other languages, like ORIAT FM, Radio Maxima, Echo Doliny, Poytakht, and others. They usually give a short overview of the world news every fifteen or thirty minutes and fill the rest of time with music and advertisements. There are also several national stations, belonging to the Uzbekistan Television and Radio Company, broadcasting in Uzbek and Russian.

NEWSPAPERS AND MAGAZINES

Uzbek newspapers and magazines can be broadly divided into two categories: special and entertaining. The first category includes publications by official administrative bodies that focus on professional issues related to their own activities. There are newspapers and journals for lawyers, tax inspectors, the police, and so on. Official newspapers published by the government, such as *Xalq So'zi* and *Jamiyat* also belong in this category. The second group includes a number of publications focusing almost exclusively on entertainment. They feature articles about local and international stars, film and book reviews, gossip and trivia, fashions, style, clothes, and gadgets, along with crosswords and other games and puzzles. Some of these are downloaded from the Internet, and some are generated locally.

INTERNET

The only true window to the outside world is the Internet. By international standards, Internet speeds are still quite low, as dial-up connections and 3G modems still predominate; even so, Internet speeds have increased almost sixfold in the past ten years. Although fiber optic cable is available as well as Wi-Fi, all communications have to go through a central hub, which allows the Internet to be monitored. The number of Internet users has risen from 1.8 million in 2007 to 11 million in 2011, but affordability is one of the factors preventing more widespread use. The country has been struggling to bring its telecom system up to international standards. The situation is gradually improving, and there has been a positive development in the country's Internet market in recent years.

TELEPHONE

It is difficult to predict how long landline phones will remain in place in Uzbekistan, as most people now use cell phones. There are five cell phone companies in the country: Beeline, UCell, and UMS, working in the GSM format, and Perfectum Mobile and UzMobile providing CDMA connection. Mobile connection in Uzbekistan is relatively cheap (around US $0.04 per day) but you have to pay around US $2 or more in advance. To get a SIM card you need to produce a local passport and registration at the company's office or in special Paynet outlets, which issue cards and accept payment in soums. To get CDMA connection you need to go to the company's office. Each company has a range of tariffs and you can always check your balance to find out how soon you will need to refill your card. You have free local calls and text messages, but texting and calling to other countries is expensive.

As everywhere in the world, smartphones have enhanced and at the same time reduced the human capacity for communication. The sight of people wearing earphones and staring at their electronic devices has become commonplace in the cities of Uzbekistan. For good or ill, this is a sure sign that the times are changing, even in a country so keen to keep its traditions alive.

MAIL

The postal service, O'zbekiston Pochtasi, has been used less and less in recent years, especially in the big cities, as most people no longer write each other letters. Some official bodies send their correspondence by post, and plenty of parcels, small packages, and registered items are mailed. Although generally reliable, delivery can be slow. Large post offices also offer courier services. In villages, the post office is still an administrative hub though no longer a social focal point.

CONCLUSION

Uzbekistan is a fascinating country inhabited by kind, open, and hospitable people, and it deserves to be better known in the world. Although recently some progress has been made in this regard and Uzbek monuments have featured in several international TV programs and publications, the country is still presented mostly as a glamorous "Oriental" place, and this is understandable. Of course, tiled minarets, bright shawls, and hot flatbreads are exotic and attractive, but there is so much more to it.

In this book, we have set out to give you an insight into the inner life of Uzbekistan and its people. It has been important to focus on the country's cultural diversity and complexity, and to highlight things that might be unfamiliar, strange, or unclear to visitors. Ultimately, *Culture Smart! Uzbekistan* is about the people who form a mosaic of different historic, ethnic, class, educational, and cultural backgrounds. While it may not be easy to navigate through all these complexities, it is definitely worth the effort. Come to Uzbekistan prepared, and you will be well rewarded!

Further Reading

Adams, Laura L. *The Spectacular State. Culture and National Identity in Uzbekistan*. Durham and London: Duke University Press, 2010.

Alexander, Christopher Aslan. *A Carpet Ride to Khiva: Seven Years on the Silk Road*. London: Icon Books Ltd, 2009.

Bissel, Tom. *Chasing the Sea. Lost Among the Ghosts of Empire in Central Asia*. New York: Vintage, 2004.

Finke, Peter. *Variations on Uzbek Identity*. New York, Oxford: Berghahn, 2014.

Hopkirk, Peter. *Setting the East Ablaze: Lenin's Dream of an Empire in Asia*. Oxford: Oxford University Press, 1984.

Hopkirk, Peter. *The Great Game. On Secret Service in High Asia*. Oxford: Oxford University Press, 2001.

Ismailov, Hamid. *The Railway*. London: Random House UK, 2008.

MacLean, Fitzroy. *Eastern Approaches*. London: Penguin Books, 1991.

Macleod, Calum, and Bradley Mayhew. *Uzbekistan: The Golden Road to Samarkand* (Odyssey Illustrated Guides). Hong Kong: Odyssey Publications, 2014.

Morrison, Alexander. *Russian Rule in Samarkand*. Oxford: Oxford University Press, 2008.

Murray, Craig. *Murder in Samarkand*. Edinburgh: Mainstream Publishing Company, 2006.

Thubron, Colin. *The Lost Heart of Asia*. New York: Vintage, 2004.

Some Useful Web Sites

UzbekistanToday
http://ut.uz/en
UzDaily.com – Uzbekistan news: business, finance, markets, statistics
https://www.uzdaily.com/
The Telegraph: Uzbekistan News
http://www.telegraph.co.uk/news/worldnews/asia/uzbekistan/
http://www.fergananews.com/
http://www.uzmetronom.com/

culture smart! uzbekistan

Index

Acknowledgments

I would like to thank Rene Fischer, Umida Akhmedova,
Catriona Gray, Umida Nurjanova, Nathan Jeffers, Muhayyo
Zairova, David Wise, Maksud Askarov, Vaughan Ross, Erik
Khisamiev, Ashot Danielyan, and Ludmila Nikitina for their
contributions and kind advice.